Rendez-vous Leicester Square

The History of Notre Dame de France 1865-2015

Isabelle Le Chevallier

Copyright © 2015 Notre Dame de France

ISBN 978-0-9932456-0-2

Publisher : Notre Dame de France,
5 Leicester Place, London WC2H 7BX
T : +4420 7437 9363.

www.ndfchurch.org

Editorial Team: Paul Walsh s.m., Anne Marie Salgo, Odile Rimbert, Francine Cronin, Nicole Paice, Marie Madelain

Translation: Edmund Duffy s.m., Kevin Mowbray s.m.

Design: Kersten Bepler, Steve Ward

Printed in the UK – Transform Management Ltd.

*Laurence Blow (1957-2014),
trustee of Notre Dame de France and
Notre Dame Refugee Centre,
launched the project of this book
but did not see it completed.
It is dedicated to her memory.*

Content

Foreword (Cardinal Philippe Barbarin)

Introduction   page 9

I. Origin and Historical Context   page 13
1. French Roots in England
2. The Arrival of the Huguenots
3. The French Quarter in Soho and Leicester Square
4. Victims of the French Revolution
5. England Welcomes the French in the 19th Century
6. The Marists
7. Cardinal Wiseman and the Foundation of Notre Dame de France

II. The First Church 1865-1940   page 29
1. Launching the Work
2. Building the Church
3. Establishing the Mission
4. An Expanding Mission
5. The Second World War

III. The Second Church: Reconstruction   page 45
1. The End of the War and the Reconstruction
2. The Decoration of the New Church
   - 2.1. The Notre-Dame-de-France Tapestry of Dom Robert
   - 2.2. The Virgin of Mercy – Bas-relief by Georges Saupique
   - 2.3. The Baptismal Font and the Ambos
   - 2.4. The Mosaic of the Nativity by Boris Anrep
   - 2.5. Preparations and Painting of the Murals by Jean Cocteau
   - Description of the Murals
     - The Annunciation
     - The Crucifixion
     - The Assumption
     - A New Lease of Life

IV. Recent Times   *page 63*
1. Growth and Changes 1960-1987
    1.1. Mauritians and the African Communities
    1.2. The Centenary 1965
    1.3. New Directions for a Parish
    1.4. The Chaplaincy of the French Lycée
    1.5. A New Wave of French in London
2. Notre Dame de France without the Marists 1987-1992
3. The Return of the Marists 1992-2015
    3.1. New Perspectives, New Engagements
    3.2 New Initiatives and Communities
    3.3 Service to the Homeless
    3.4. The Notre Dame Refugee Centre
    3.5. The School Chaplaincy
    3.6. Presence and Evangelisation in the West End
    3.7. A Parish with a Difference

Afterword   *page 85*

Endnotes   *page 87*

The Rectors of Notre Dame de France   *page 97*

Bibliography   *page 98*

The Parish of Notre Dame de France in London

Did you know that the roots of the Society of Mary are embedded in Lyons? It was in Lyons itself that Jean Claude Colin and Marcellin Champagnat were ordained deacons (along with a certain Jean-Marie Vianney, on the 23rd June 1815, almost 200 years ago) and on the very same day, just one year later in 1816, they were ordained priests. Little by little, as a plaque in the ancient chapel of Fourvière points out, they entrusted to the Virgin Mary their plan for a congregation consecrated to the missions. So, two decades later, it was no surprise to find a parish in London called Notre Dame de France, administered by the Fathers of the new congregation.

The aim of this book is to describe in detail how the parish developed the mission entrusted to it from its foundation in 1865 until the present day.

We learn that the French presence grew in London especially through the waves of immigration of Protestants, and then Catholics, – at the time of the Reformation, after the Revocation of the Edict of Nantes, during the French Revolution, – which turned London into a place of asylum. The French quarter in Soho, which has existed since the time of the Huguenot refugees, welcomed the newcomers who arrived destitute throughout the 19th century and tried to respond to their most urgent needs.

In the 1860s, a prominent English personality was to leave his mark on the future of the little colony. This was the very pastorally-minded Cardinal Wiseman, first Archbishop of Westminster, who realised the necessity of erecting a parish and building a church for the French Catholic community. It was he who made an appeal to the recently founded Society of Mary, as well as to the Work of the Propagation of the Faith (with origins also in Lyons through Pauline Jaricot's efforts) which played a major role in the financial support of Catholic missions throughout the world. Apart from the church, dedicated to Our Lady of Victories, the new parish had a boys' school, a girls' school, a crèche and an orphanage, all of which had to be financed. When Father Faure, founder and first parish priest of Notre Dame de France, retired in 1881 the mission had been well established – providing "*the help of schooling, charity and religion*" for the French immigrants.

In the decades which followed the Notre Dame de France community continued to do whatever was asked of it. During the 1914-1918 war it developed works of charity for the benefit of the soldiers. In 1920, when the French Lycée was created, Marist Fathers were appointed chaplains and they soon afterwards began a branch of the scout movement. Welcoming, listening and reaching out were the three characteristics which sum up the focus of the parish throughout the years. During the Second World War the parish paid a heavy toll as a result of the bombings but continued to serve as best it could. After the war lay people played a major role in rebuilding the church, establishing charitable works, spiritual and cultural activities. The 1960s saw the arrival of another wave of immigrants coming from Commonwealth countries, from Mauritius, Congo and from the Ivory Coast, making Notre Dame de France a truly multicultural community. At the time of the centenary celebration in 1965 the community presented itself as a vital and active one, along the lines of the recently concluded second Vatican Council. Further developments in that same spirit were the ecumenical meetings with the Anglican community.

During a short period (1987-1992) when there were no Marists in residence, due to a shortage of manpower in the congregation, parish life slowed down. Once a new team of Marists returned it was possible to focus again on the key objectives: responding to the needs of the Catholic Francophone community and getting involved pastorally in the local neighbourhood. The call to assist the homeless and the ever increasing number of asylum seekers mobilised numerous volunteers, activities located in the former school which is now the parish centre (Peter Chanel Centre).

What else would you expect? As Notre Dame de France celebrates its 150th anniversary in 2015, it continues to draw inspiration from Marist spirituality and its tradition of welcoming all and caring for people in need, especially the most destitute. It captures a slice of the history of our Church and of France. It finds itself very much in line with the direction given by Pope Francis in his exhortation "The Joy of the Gospel": *if the Church exists it is in order to evangelise. Instead of simple administration it should establish everywhere a permanent state of mission.*

I am glad that I was invited to write the preface to this fine work. I wish to express my gratitude and that of the Church of France for the vitality of Notre Dame de France, which is evident in the welcome given to a good number of families from my parishes and my successive dioceses, and the spiritual nourishment generously offered to them over many decades. Allow me to place the writer and the readers of this book under the protection of Our Lady of Fourvière at whose feet I write these lines on this Feast of St. Joseph.

Notre Dame de Fourvière, Notre Dame de France pray for us!

Cardinal Philippe Barbarin
19th March 2015

Introduction

In 2015 the church of Notre Dame de France celebrates its 150th anniversary. The aim of this brief history is to describe the roots of the Francophone community which worships there and the growth and development of its mission in the heart of London from its beginnings in the middle of the 19th century until the present-day.

The Francophone community in London now constitutes one of the largest groups of foreigners in the city. It currently numbers more than 300,000. To briefly recount how such a large community of immigrants came to exist is the purpose of the first chapter. It describes their arrival from France in several waves from the time of William the Conqueror's invasion of England in the 11th century until the middle of the 19th century. It also recalls how Soho and Leicester Square, popular places of entertainment even in the 18th century, became the "French Quarter" of London. In this way the reasons for the present location of the church in Soho and for its design are made clear.

The second chapter gives an account of the foundation of Notre Dame de France in 1865 and its growth until 1940. Archbishop Wiseman, the first Archbishop of Westminster after the official re-establishment of the Catholic hierarchy in 1850, was moved by the situation of the poverty stricken French immigrants living in and near London's Leicester Square. So he called on the French Marists, who were already active in the East End of London, to come to the aid of their fellow citizens. In 1865 Father Charles Faure began the mission which is still in the care of the Marists to this day. Father Faure quickly began a comprehensive mission consisting of a church, a boys' school, a girls' school, an orphanage, a crèche and a hospital. He was also responsible for the construction of the first church which was designed by Auguste Boileau, one of the pioneers in the use of cast-iron in architecture. The years following the departure of Father Faure saw numerous rectors come and go. More disruptive though was the impact of the First and Second World Wars. From 1914 until 1945 the church and community of Notre Dame de France experienced extraordinary change. These troubled though vibrant years, culminating in the destruction of the church during the Blitz, are also mentioned in this chapter.

The years after the destruction of the church in the Blitz are recounted in the third chapter. After the war Notre Dame de France was rebuilt by the architect Hubert Corfiato following the contours of the first church. The church reopened its doors in 1955 looking just like it is today. Over a period of a few years it was decorated as a showcase of contemporary French art on the recommendation of René Varin, then cultural attaché to the embassy. Tourists and music lovers are still attracted by the murals of Jean Cocteau, the Aubusson tapestry woven according to the drawings of the Benedictine Dom Robert de Chaunac, the mosaics of Boris Anrep, the sculptures of Georges Saupique and finally a Cavaillé-Coll organ restored to its original French tone. The numerous pastoral works of the Marists during these years are also mentioned. Some of these were founded in the aftermath of the First World War; others were initiatives after the Second World War. Many of them still continue today.

The fourth and final chapter describes Notre Dame de France from the 1960s until the present day emphasizing the diversity and complexity of its constantly growing mission. The Marist team itself now reflects this diversity and complexity. From the time of Father Faure the Marist team had always attempted to be creatively faithful to the vision and mission of their Founder, Father Jean-Claude Colin. This meant discerning how best to serve the community of Notre Dame de France in a rapidly changing world, whilst paying special attention to young people and their education in the faith. So when the Marists returned to Notre Dame de France in 1992, after five years absence (1987-1992), they drew on their membership from around the world to make a new team which was international in character with a wider mandate: not only to continue providing for the pastoral needs of the French and Francophone communities but also to extend the mission to the church's surrounding neighbourhood.

This wider mandate is reflected in the numerous charitable activities which are now based in the parish. A refugee centre has been opened for displaced persons who come from all corners of the world. A weekly food service for the poor and homeless which began in 1933 still continues. Accommodation is provided for the homeless during winter nights. Pastoral counselling is offered in the church where there is a welcoming room.

Diversity and complexity also describes the community which gathers at Notre Dame de France. Once clearly *French* in character, now it could be more properly described as a *Francophone* parish. Many immigrants from French-speaking nations who have settled in London have been welcomed as new members in the community: Mauritians first of all, then Congolese, followed by those from the Ivory Coast and many other African countries. Today more than half of those coming to Notre Dame de France on a regular basis are Francophone Africans who have formed very many groups for reflection and prayer.

The mission to young people remains focussed on the French Lycée, the spiritual direction of which has been entrusted to the Marists based at Notre Dame de France for over one hundred years. There are now approximately 1,000 children under the care of about one hundred volunteers. The catechism classes and the various activities are spread around different areas in London but all the children and their families come together to receive the sacraments in Notre Dame de France, the heart of the parish.

The history of Notre Dame de France shows continuity in the midst of discontinuity – constant presence and service which is always open to a world that is forever changing. It tells of various initiatives taken to address new situations and demands. All that remains possible thanks to the ever increasing participation of volunteers, the regular collaboration with the Catholic parishes of the neighbourhood and the call to evangelise which is at the heart of the Marist vocation.

Isabelle Le Chevallier

INTRODUCTION 11

I. Origin and Historical Context

1. French Roots in England

William the Conqueror's victory over England in 1066 had lasting consequences. While still having to deal with frequent conflicts between them, the rulers of England and France quickly established solid, commercial relationships. England, for example, exported the best quality wool to the continent and France, in turn, the finest wines to England. In fact, the Gascon wine merchants were the first French to establish themselves as a group in London from the 12th century onwards.

For the next three centuries the English kings, from Henry II Plantagenet to Henry VI of Lancaster, married into French royalty.[1] With each marriage they received an entire court of lords, churchmen, intellectuals, masons, and craftsmen. Numerous Monastic Orders (Benedictines, Cluniac, Cistercians and Augustinians) also came from the continent during this period and founded abbeys and monasteries. These regular arrivals influenced the spread of French culture and language. So great was this influence that French soon replaced Latin as the cultural language of reference, – for example, teaching was done in French at Oxford University until 1349.[2]

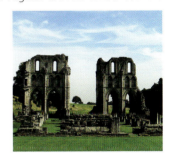

By the beginning of the 16th century, the Church owned more than a fifth of the land in England. In London the strength of the Church was even more pronounced – over half of the territory of the city was occupied by monasteries and religious establishments! However, there was an abrupt change in this situation in 1538. Against the will of the pope Henry VIII had set up the Anglican reform in 1529. He had done this in order that he could annul his first marriage and so facilitate his second marriage. Then, by the Acts of 1533 and 1534 the country had become schismatic without, however, joining the Protestant Reformation. Consequently, in 1538 Henry ordered the dissolution of monasteries. In 1559 Elizabeth I became Supreme Governor of the Church of England.

Under the Stuart dynasty the court remained French in character. Charles I had married Princess Henrietta-Marie, sister of Louis XIII. This made the future Charles II a first cousin of Louis XIV. However, royal absolutism in England effectively disappeared forever with the execution of Charles I who was beheaded on the 30th January 1649. At the end of the 17th century "*there is no control of religion as in Catholic France; the more attenuated royal power interferes less in religious matters in London than in Paris*".[3]

The *Glorious Revolution*[4] of 1688, which put William III, the sworn enemy of Louis XIV, on the throne in a relatively bloodless coup, changed the tone of the relations between England and France. In 1689, for example, William and Mary, his wife, publicly supported French Calvinist refugees and created a *charity fund*[5] for them.

England welcomed these refugees with open arms – not only because England had become fiercely anti-Catholic, but also because the country benefitted politically and economically. The refugees, imbued with strong Calvinist values, were highly skilled and had a well-developed business spirit.[6] These *Huguenots* were the first wave of French refugees to arrive in London. Many of them settled there permanently.

2. The Arrival of the Huguenots

The French Church in Hog Lane, Soho. William Hogarth, Four Times of the Day, Noon.

In the 16th century Elizabeth I had made her country a place of asylum and a retirement base for protestant reformers who sought to leave France. The first of them[7] came over to England[8] to escape religious persecution. Protected by the English sovereigns,[9] they would continue to come in ever greater numbers after the St. Bartholomew Massacre in 1572. The majority were rich, middle-class people, lawyers or doctors, all of whom were busy forming solid networks of influence with the powers that be.

The Revocation of the *Edict of Nantes* in 1685 suppressed the freedom of religion: the Huguenots had to become Catholics or risk their lives in the galleys. This new law sent over 200,000 Huguenots on their way to countries of refuge.[10] Of the 50,000 *religious refugees* who chose England and the British Isles about half of them preferred London where more than twenty protestant places of worship were established for them. This second wave was made up of artisians, merchants and tradesmen: shopkeepers or craftsmen with remarkable skills in printing, watchmaking, metal work, both in ordinary or precious metal, and arms manufacturing. They excelled as weavers, particularly in processing silk[11] and manufacturing ribbons. In fact, soon after the Great Fire of 1666 such craftsmen had begun to revive Spitalfields in the East End, an area outside the ramparts of the city which was controlled by the exclusive and powerful *Guilds*.[12] In this way London became the new textile capital of Europe, producing the finest silks according to the techniques invented in Tours and Lyons.

The integration of the Huguenots was swift and permanent. Before the end of the 18th century, they occupied the most enviable places in politics, diplomacy, the army, medical science, law, and were among the founders of the *Bank of England*. Others were intellectuals or famous artists.

3. The French Quarter in Soho and Leicester Square

The Huguenots, who arrived in London during the reign of Louis XIV, were the first occupants of the recently built houses west of Covent Garden in the north of Leicester Fields. This new quarter was called Soho. It was also soon to become known as the *French Quarter*. The French occupied more than eight hundred houses there. Everything was done in French: school classes, business affairs, official registers and also religious services.

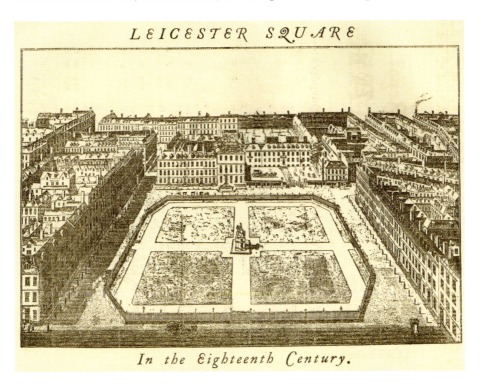

At the beginning of the 17th century there was scarcely any trace of urbanisation in and around St. Martin in the Fields. But the situation changed after 1630 when Robert Sidney, Count of Leicester, acquired land in the parish. In the north-east of his property he organised the construction of a large house[13] and closed off the space in front of his residence, thus barring access to what used to be a public passageway. The parishioners affected by this loss

ORIGIN AND HISTORICAL CONTEXT

of access referred the matter to the king.[14] As a consequence Lord Leicester was obliged to reopen a part of his property which was known from then on as *Leicester Fields*. In due time this was to become *Leicester Square*.

Twenty years later an elegant area had been established around Leicester House. It was much sought after by the aristocracy and ambassadors. In 1688, Charles Colbert de Croissy,[15] the French Ambassador, lived in Leicester House and maintained a Catholic chapel under his roof. So Catholic liturgies were already being celebrated in London in a French chapel at the very place where the Marist Fathers, almost two centuries later, would establish Notre Dame de France!

For a while Leicester House became a royal residence. First the daughter[16] of James I lived there. Later Frederic of Hanover, elector Prince and Prince of Wales,[17] also lived in it with his family. Voltaire, who resided in England from 1726-29, was so enthusiastic about this fashionable and refined area that he wrote of it *"Had I been a gentleman of leisure, I would have chosen Leicester Square as my birth place"*.[18]

The area did not prosper for very long. Around 1770, Leicester House ceased to be a royal residence. It was soon sold and consequently became an exhibition house for a collection of natural and ethnological curiosities.[19] It was the beginning of a swift and irreversible decline, despite the presence of renowned personalities and artists installed[20] around the Square. In 1791 the banker, Thomas Wright, took over what was left of Leicester House and its gardens. He demolished the house, unoccupied since 1788, and made a new entrance into Leicester Place which was a little street joining Lisle Street and the north-east of Leicester Square.

At the beginning of the 19th century the houses which had been constructed and occupied by the first Huguenots in Soho were no longer well maintained as their descendants had moved to better quarters. The occupants grouped around Leicester Square were still French but of more modest means, the majority being tradesmen. From then on Leicester Square became known as a place for strolling and popular entertainment.

Popular entertainments in Leicester Square

James Wyld's[21] *Great Terrestrial Globe* enjoyed a vivid and brief success at the time of the *Great Exposition* in 1851 at Crystal Palace. The public moved around the interior of an empty globe[22] with the aid of ladders linked up with platforms at different levels. In this way, with the help of plaster models which reproduced mountains and rivers made to scale, they were able to marvel at the geography of the whole world.

On the east side of the square the *Royal Panopticon of Arts and Sciences* opened its doors in the spring of 1854. Created to serve as a window for the new artistic and scientific achievements, the huge building[23] closed down after two years and became the Alhambra music-hall theatre.

The rotunda which housed the *Royal Panorama*, was constructed by the painter Robert Baker[24] in 1791 in the north-east corner of the square on the site of the *Feathers Inn*, so named in memory of the Prince of Wales who was a former resident of Leicester House.

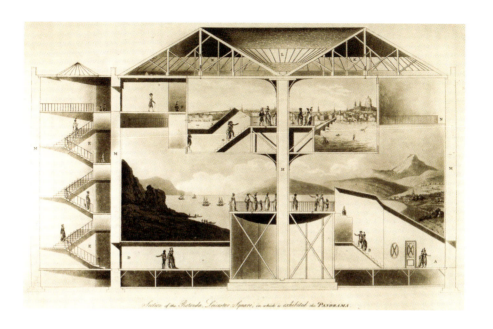

What is a Panorama?

In 1787, Robert Baker took out a patent for his invention (*Nature in the blink of an eye*) under the name of *Panorama*.[25] All through the 18th century the keen desire of the public to see and to know more revealed itself both in a thirst for the curious and a slowly growing taste for the *picturesque*.

The Panorama used different optical tricks offering spectators the illusion of being at the heart of the action. Entering the rotunda through a dark passageway fitted with natural overhead lighting, the visitor had a view of the Panorama[26] from a central platform surrounded by a railing. A 360 degree naturalistic painting,[27] big enough to give the spectator the impression of being part of the scene represented, was exhibited in a rotunda built for this purpose. Through a play of perspectives and lighting, with additional shadows on the side to increase the impression of depth, the effect of being immersed in the spectacle was gripping. Such panoramas had no visible borders and seemed to keep unrolling endlessly.

The rotunda in Leicester Square was the first of its kind and the only one presenting two panoramas, one on top of the other. Two observation platforms were necessary but this brought in twice as much money. The first 360 degree panorama shown in the rotunda[28] was a view of London from Albion Mills. The first panoramas showed views of the town where the panoramas were. Later battles on land or on sea become the most popular themes.

ORIGIN AND HISTORICAL CONTEXT 17

4. Victims of the French Revolution

The Revolution and the years of Terror prompted a new influx of French refugees into England. Now, however, the immigrants were Catholics. There were as many as 20,000 of them. First, from 1789 onwards, the Bourbon princes and the grand aristocracy arrived in London transporting their "houses" and their carefree life style with them to the new quarter of Marylebone, north of Oxford Street. The following year another wave of immigration began but this time it was "...*soldiers, sailors, intellectuals, journalists, craftsmen and middle-class merchants who shared high society's fidelity to the king"*.[29]

After the introduction of the *Civil Constitution of the Clergy*,[30] which divided the latter into jurors (*constitutional clergy*) or non-jurors (*resistants*), half of the priests and almost all of the bishops[31] in France were to flee. The records of the English Customs reveal that in the first three weeks of 1792 more than 4,000 French priests disembarked in the ports of the south of England. By 1795 this number had increased to 10,000! Some provided for their needs by becoming professors in colleges, private tutors in families, employees in workshops of the clothing industry or in printing. The majority survived thanks to the assistance of the Catholics in London and the subsidies[32] voted by the English government which granted a shilling a day to the unfortunates.

For these thousands of priests, however, there were not enough churches in which to say mass. In London many said mass in their rooms or their dormitory without liturgical vestments or candles. Masses succeeded one after the other on every available altar in the Catholic chapels of the missions in the area or in the Embassies. Other masses were said in the French room of the *Middlesex Hospital* in Soho where twenty or so sick priests were being cared for by the French nuns. For the most part English Protestants showed great generosity towards the French refugees. They multiplied private initiatives in their favour, organised collections during their religious services and created many relief committees and welcoming centres.

Not everybody had good feelings towards the immigrants. While the aristocrats were welcomed easily by their British peers the less well-to-do refugees, who were arriving from France in ever greater numbers, gave rise to protests and jealousy. When both countries went to war[33] again, *The Alien Act*[34] came into force in order to prevent the infiltration of undesirable elements. This Act obliged new arrivals to register at their port of entry, to notify the authorities of their address and to report their movements.

From 1792 to 1815 a dozen chapels were created for those priests and the civilian immigrants who had no church. The first was in Soho which once more became *the French Quarter* where all sorts of French immigrants mingled and spoke only in French. The Huguenot tradesmen who worked there showed great kindness to the refugees, even though they were Catholics.

The most destitute of the civilians and the poorest priests lived south of the Thames.[35] *Notre Dame Chapel* was founded for them. In 1801 another larger one was dedicated to St. Louis. The latter was closed a year later when more and more priests returned to France after the vote on the *Concordat of 1801*.[36] This Concordat recognised the Catholic faith as the religion of the majority in the country.

Some chapels constructed for the French eventually became English Catholic parishes but the majority disappeared when the immigrants returned to the continent, during the short interruption of the Anglo-French hostilities after the Treaty of Amiens.[37] The only one left was the tiny church of Little George Street, near Portman Square, consecrated in 1799 under the name of Our Lady of the Annunciation. It served as a refuge for the representatives of the various dynasties dethroned by the successive revolutions in France. It finally closed permanently in 1911.

5. England Welcomes the French in the 19th Century

French immigrants arrived in a steady flow throughout the 19th century. London, in particular, continued to prove attractive to them. Sometimes it was because they were in danger in France, sometimes they wanted to try their luck in the big city which was being transformed by the industrial revolution and sometimes it was because they just sought a life of peace and quiet.

After 1803 about 1,000 French priests and many thousands of civilians chose to stay on in London. For almost fifteen years[38] chapels continued to be built for them in Chelsea, Hampstead or Westminster. The poor who could not afford to return to France, where nothing awaited them, crowded around Leicester Square and constituted the core of what was then called *the French colony*. It was for them that the work of Notre Dame was founded.

The French in London before 1860

In the first half of the 19th century the French population in London was made up of many different groups. There were about 50,000 working individuals recorded in the *Commercial Year Book of the French in England*,[39] most of whom lived in London. The official census of the capital allows us to give more precise details. For the most part the men were artists (i.e. actors, musicians or painters) merchants and cooks. There were also wine merchants, hatters and shoemakers. Many of the women were in professions to do with fashion, such as clothes designers, glove makers and milliners or with household management such as governesses, servants and nannies. One must also add some forty French hotel owners around Leicester Square accommodating 30,000 compatriots who crossed the English Channel every year.

There were also refugees, political outlaws, and all sorts of opponents of the monarchy – Bonapartists in 1815, legitimist Royalists in 1830, Orleanists in 1848, Republicans (forty-eighters),[40] anarchists, then "communards" in 1871, all keeping a low profile and delighted to find anonymity in the greatest city of the world.

The rapidly[41] expanding metropolis was home to many other French citizens who had no profession and had no intention of finding one, a whole population at odds with society – ex-convicts and small time con men, deserters, bankrupts, marginalised or those who were seduced by the new ideologies and became political activists.

Poorer still were the street vendors, the unemployed who survived with difficulty and many families without any resources. They were crammed into unhealthy lodgings around Leicester Square which at that time was one of the worst quarters in London.

The more fortunate French were moved by the misery of their compatriots. The Embassy and the Consulate did what was possible to save the "*strayed subjects*" amidst the "*faithless and the lawless*". In 1842, Alfred d'Orsay founded The French Society of Charity.[42] Two years later the Catholics of the English parish of Warwick Street created the first *Conference of St. Vincent de Paul* in England.[43] With a view to "raising the moral standards of the French in Leicester Square" the descendants of the first Huguenots, now part of English Protestant society, founded the *Poor Man's Guardian Society* and opened a soup kitchen in the basement of Leicester Square. Apart from those who lived where they worked, nearly all the French lived in Soho. An English author[44] of the time wrote of Soho: "*We see there a modern, filthy France swarming with waiters, linen maids, rich and poor French alike.*"

They all had their own way of getting by in this quarter where everyone knew everyone else: "*if the French police were looking for someone they had a good chance of finding him playing dominos in a café in Soho or stamping his feet to keep warm in the evening in Regent Street*".[45] "*They stayed at the Hotel de Seine in King Street, met at the Café de la Sablonnière in Leicester Square or had dinner at Chez Victor in Old Compton Street. Most of the commercial business was run by the French.*"[46]

Through the initiatives of Dr Vintras and the great perfumer, Rimmel, the *French Dispensary*[47] was created in Regent Street in 1861. In the same year the project for a new French mission to be established in the Soho quarter was announced publicly. In London there were many rich French people like those who used the church of Little George Street near Portman Square. This was the only place of worship, built by and for the French immigrants at the end of the 18th century, which was still in use. The chapel was situated a half hour's walk from Soho and the parish priest,[49] when consulted, said he was too old to undertake the task. No one could really expect him to help the French in Leicester Square who had no links with the elegant congregation he was used to mixing with!

Cardinal Wiseman,[50] the first Archbishop of Westminster after the Catholic hierarchy[51] was re-established in England and Wales, understood the urgent necessity to establish a new mission for the French community in Soho. One of the priorities of the new Archbishop was to found national parishes which would take care of the numerous foreign Catholics in his diocese: Polish, German, Italians and, in particular, the Irish in the East End. The Great Famine in the 1840s, due to the failure[52] of the potato crop, had brought a flood of Irish immigrants who crammed into the slums near the docks. It was to support this particularly impoverished community that Cardinal Wiseman had already solicited the help of the very young Society of Mary.[53]

6. The Marists

France had been de-Christianised by the anticlerical movements resulting from the revolution. At the beginning of the 19th century it began to experience a renewal of religious fervour[54] which brought about the creation of numerous congregations and religious orders. A lively enthusiasm for the missionary cause soon made France the principal home of Catholic missions. From the time of the restoration of the monarchy giving to the missions became widely popular thanks to the regular solicitation of very small donations – a cent each week – initiated by Pauline Jaricot,[55] foundress of the work of *The Propagation of the Faith* in Lyons in 1822. In the 19th century Lyons was to become both the financial capital of the missions and the world's greatest information centre on the missions.

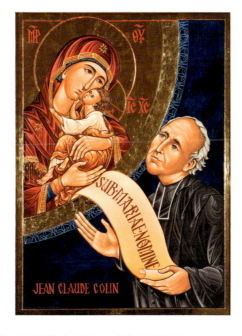

The Bulletin of the Works of the Propagation of the Faith spread missionary stories very quickly and so, for the first time in the history of the Church, echoes of the struggles of missionaries reached the remotest of villages in Catholic Europe, enthralling old and young alike. Thus fervour to support the missions grew and grew to match the ever-increasing numbers of religious men and women leaving Europe for distant lands.

Founded in Lyons *"to respond to the great needs of the peoples"*, the fathers and brothers of the Society of Mary (the Marists) committed themselves particularly to assist the poor, the young and the foreign missions.

The Society of Mary was conceived as a family with four branches uniting Fathers, Brothers, Sisters and a Third Order of lay people bonded together by the same spiritual ideal – to be like Mary at the service of the Church through efficacious but discreet work. In 1836 Pope Gregory XVI officially approved the Society and entrusted to it the mission to evangelise the islands of the Western Oceania. In the same year the first twenty Marist Fathers took their vows and Father Colin was elected the first Superior General. On Christmas Eve of 1836 the first group of missionaries set sail for the Pacific.

Given the number of new missions that were established in the British colonies of New Zealand and Australia, it was thought necessary to set up in London a *mission centre* for the French missionaries in transit. There they would be able to learn the language and organise, on the spot, arrangements for transport and funding. It was in this way that the Marist presence in London began around 1840. Their first mission there was in Whitechapel, led by Father Charles Chaurain.

7. Cardinal Wiseman and the Foundation of Notre Dame de France

Cardinal Wiseman

Cardinal Wiseman was impressed by the success of St. Anne's parish in Spitalfields, where the Marist team had built a church and a school for the Irish. He made a further appeal to the Society of Mary in 1860[57] to *"organise a mission or a Catholic parish for their compatriots near where they were and to build a centre there for charitable and religious works similar to what the French had in their own country."*[58] Father Charles Faure,[59] former teacher and missionary in France who had left St. Anne's parish in 1857, became the founder of this new mission.

The needs were enormous but the project was not approved of by all. The Portland Square parish viewed unfavourably a second charitable work in London and the French Embassy refused to acknowledge the numbers and the poverty of the French in Leicester Square. Some *good souls* claimed that it was undermining the ministry of the French-speaking English priests.

Undeterred Father Faure went everywhere: he visited the poorest families and the sick in the area; he went to the other Catholic parishes in Soho; he preached the Lenten sermons in Portland Square church; he also made many approaches to influential ecclesiastics in Westminster Diocese and to the official French authorities. Alone, however, without resources or an office, he could not achieve very much.

While on a visit to Paris, in 1860, he went to Our Lady of Victories Church.[60] The renewal of that church seemed to be a model to follow. It had been returned to the Catholic Church for worship in 1809 but was very poorly attended for years. However, when the parish priest[61] decided to consecrate the church to the Heart of Mary it experienced an extraordinary revival. In 1860, it became a fervent centre of Marian devotion and thousands of names were enrolled on its registers. Father Faure decided to take inspiration from Our Lady of Victories for the future church in London, itself dedicated to Mary. As well he wanted the church to be "*a gentle oasis for lost souls and, in addition, to present a vision of the absent Motherland*". He wished to begin schools, a hospital and a hostel with the St. Vincent of Paul Sisters. His plan was approved by Cardinal Wiseman but, unfortunately, all the cardinal could offer was advice: "*If I had gold or silver I would be happy to offer it to you for such a huge project... But let France know the true situation!*"[62]

Father Faure made several trips to France to speak about the Notre Dame de France project to the French Bishops, armed with a letter from the Cardinal: "*My Lord, we have resolved to establish in London, a project worthy of all the sympathy of France and of the illustrious Bishops of this great nation. The aim of Notre Dame de France*

is to support, in their faith and their virtuous living, thousands of French who reside in London and who are exposed continuously to every seduction imaginable. Lend us your support, my Lord, with your eloquent words and the fervour of your apostolic heart. Father Faure, to whom I have given responsibility for this project, will present you with all the documents you can desire".[63] All means possible were used to inform the French on the continent and to encourage donations – personal visits, conferences, sermons, jumble sales, and distribution of flyers.

Cardinal Wiseman eventually overcame all resistance from the authorities. On several occasions he personally asked for help from "*The Work of the Propagation of the Faith*".[64]

> "*Mr. President*, Among all the sad things a Catholic regrets to find in London, the saddest, undeniably, is the moral and religious state of the French living in the capital of England. Isn't it about time that the Church in France showed her children in London that she is their true mother? I ardently desire to bring back to the path of salvation these children of France that Providence has entrusted to me. This hugely important project has already received the most abundant blessings of the Sovereign Pontiff Pius X and has just been welcomed in Paris by H.E. Cardinal Archbishop…It is true; there are churches in London and excellent French priests or priests who know French. In spite of having these religious aids our French have fallen into the state in which we now see them. These aids are insufficient. What is lacking, therefore, is a French, Catholic charitable organisation especially intended for the French in the Leicester Square quarter. They need a church in their vicinity which is always accessible. They need missionaries who are always ready to receive them and go out and visit them in their humble homes. They need teachers to instruct the children and fill their hearts with love of their religion and love of France. They need works of charity to save a large number of young girls who have been lured by illusions and had their hopes quickly dissipated in this dangerous capital. They need Sisters again, to help the poor, to visit and take care of the sick and console the dying! … At this time, however, practically all our concern is about the church and, even more especially, to get a plot of land spacious enough on which to build. Housing for the Brothers and Sisters or a residence for the Missionaries are much less of a worry than the church. Why? Because the Christian Brothers want to open schools at their own expense, some charitable people from Paris have undertaken to provide a house for the Sisters, and a few small rented rooms will do as a residence for the missionaries… Once we have the land the work would go ahead and, that being the case, it wouldn't be imprudent to open a temporary chapel in the French quarter. After that it would just be a matter of waiting for Providence to indicate when to start building the Church and then we could, in all confidence, solicit the help of the English. We were told that we could get land in the centre of London if we had from 80 to 100,000 francs. Providence has already procured a third of that amount…*"*[65]

For three years the Notre Dame project would constantly meet obstacles which could have delayed or even stopped it altogether. Then, at long last, encouraging news arrived in the spring of 1864:

> *"On the 20th April* a property in Leicester Square with a lease for 27 years was put up for auction. The property consisted of the following:
>
> 1. A large circular construction 90 feet in diameter and 70 feet high[66] known as a Panorama.
>
> 2. Two houses: one had large reading rooms; situated on the same site; intercommunication was possible; two valuable paintings[67] costing 50,000 francs were included in the sale.
>
> Since the last bidder offered only 72,500 francs, the property was still up for sale. The notary thought that with a few thousand more it could be bought. To the selling price was added an annual rent of 3,425 francs. The Panorama could easily be transformed into a suitable and spacious church. This would have the advantage of being able to receive the French free or nearly, and charge the English for seats, thus getting revenue for the upkeep of the church. The two houses were rented out and brought in 4,000 francs annually. It was thought that these houses would be suitable for schools, for the Sisters or for mission personnel. We can, I hope, raise 40,000 francs soon, taking into account a small allowance promised by the government. 20-25,000 francs would save the project. The remainder could probably be found in London, given such a speedy and complete success."[68]

The survey of the future church's site was encouraging: *"The building seems a substantial construction and strong enough to last... There is but little to undo inside the Panorama building except removing the stage on which the pictures are erected. There are no walls, galleries or pillars to pull down."*

The weeks passed and the demand for funds increased, but Providence seemed to offer an opportunity not to be missed:

> *"Mr President,* I am happy to leave the future of this project in your hands. Please let us know if you can grant us 30-35,000 francs and we will begin immediately the necessary procedures to acquire these buildings. We have just received the sad news confirming all that we knew of the dreadful moral and religious state of the French colony. All the English newspapers have revealed our losses and our shame at the Big Bazaar in St. James' Hall which was held in May to help the French Protestant Mission. That overflow of proselytising obliges us to open, at once, a church, schools and a poorhouse for the French Catholics... At the moment only the lease for 27 years is for sale, but in view of

the thousands of Catholics surrounded by the rising flood waters, can we reject the offer of giving them the ark of salvation? We have every reason to believe that the owner will not refuse either the prolongation of the lease or the sale of the site itself. The lease of the panorama and the adjacent buildings would cost approximately 80,000 francs payable in 3 months and 3,435 francs annually. The expert's report shows that the buildings are in good enough condition. The architect assumes that a sum of 25-30,000 francs would be enough to adapt them to their new purpose. The plan of the Panorama lends itself marvellously well to the new project. The rotunda will become a Church. The adjoining buildings which are quite large will do for the work of the Sisters and the schools."[70]

On the 20th July 1864, The Work of the Propagation of the Faith gave a favourable answer and promised the Westminster Diocese and the Archbishop an exceptional allocation of 30,000 francs which was urgently needed for the Notre Dame de France mission. *"The mission's best friend ever, the Archbishop,*[71] *came to see the Panorama. He was delighted with the size of the site and the advantages to be had from the other big buildings which fitted in so well. He urged us to speed up the work".*[72]

On the 25th March 1865, the Feast of the Annunciation Father Faure had Charles Walter, an intermediary and friend, sign the lease, thus making Father Faure the tenant of the Burford Panorama[73] along with an adjacent building located in number 5 Leicester Square. The lease cost £2,900 and it expired on 27th September 1890. The Panorama became Notre Dame de France.

II. The First Church 1865-1940

1. Launching the Work

Having acquired the site for the church Father Faure now had to build it. Since the launch of the project he hadn't missed out on any lead to encourage an enthusiastic outburst of national and international solidarity: " ...*For this work, intended for the French or Flemish speaking residents in London, the support of Catholic nations is needed ....Belgium, France, Switzerland, Italy, Poland and America...*"[74]

Father Faure had already received the Apostolic Blessing of Pius IX and indulgences in favour of the project. In 1865 the French government granted a subsidy of 15,000 francs. Napoleon III, who had declared his intention to give a subscription, promised 5,000 francs[75] and the Empress gave the same amount.

Father Faure

All the gifts were entered into a notebook, from the least to the most generous. These included donations from the Sovereigns and members of the Royal family, the Archbishop of Paris, the President of the Senate and other distinguished persons, as well as 2 francs from the Autun Carmelites and 3 francs "*equivalent to Jean Viala's daily earnings*".

In a letter authorising the construction, the Archbishop of Westminster made a solemn promise: "*The church and its works will be destined in perpetuity to the French population of London*".[76]

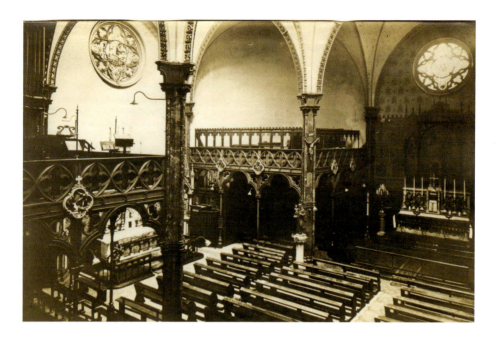

2. Building the Church

The work of adapting the old Panorama was given to Louis-Auguste Boileau,[77] one of the French pioneers in cast-iron architecture.[78] He was well-known for the use of iron frames in the construction of churches. This technique was something entirely new because until then iron structures had been reserved for buildings intended for industrial use or for markets.[79] Thanks to Boileau's innovative techniques and his use of materials which excluded traditional masonry work the construction of the French church in Leicester Square would cost less and be built more quickly.

Since the reconstruction and decoration of Westminster Parliament building by Charles Barry[80] and his associate Pugin, neo-gothic style had prevailed in civil and religious architecture throughout England. So, it must needs be used for the interior of the church which Boileau envisaged in the form of a Greek cross. According to his plan "*It boasted four independent galleries which were resting on the brick perimeter [of the old Panorama] and on the four central, iron columns. These latter supported the diagonal ribs up to the vault which constituted the essential element of the neo-gothic decoration of the interior with its ribs of broken arches above the gothic motifs of the galleries*".

In May, the site of the future Church was cleared and the work began with the solemn laying of the first stone, which would be used as the main base for one of the great pillars. Boileau came to London just once to measure the site and did not visit again until the day of the inauguration. The job was given to the local engineering contractor, A. Sauvee.[82] It was he who carried out the plan of the architect and the assembly of the metal frame. He also designed the entrance porch to Leicester Place.

It was not possible, though, to await the end of the construction work before opening a place of worship, with annexes, which was badly needed. And so, on the 8th December 1865, a provisional chapel which had been set up at the old entrance of the Panorama[83] was opened by Archbishop Manning. He was the new Archbishop of Westminster following the death of Cardinal Wiseman in February. "*There is not the least display in the temporary chapel which is small, the sanctuary being hung with crimson cloth and the altar is surmounted by a figure of Our Lady of Victories while on each side are figures of St. Joseph and St. Vincent de Paul...*"[84] Very quickly the chapel became too small as the number of Sunday worshippers soon reached 250.

Notre Dame de France, 6 Leicester Place, London, W.C.

In April 1868 "*The new church, Notre Dame de France, was almost finished... Visitors admired its elegant proportions and its slender columns, its delicate archways, its French stamp. It still lacked what would make it glorious: three altars,[85] windows, and finally the fine Stations of the Cross... All of these beautiful things came from France and are a credit to the charity of our country...*"[86]

Finally, on the 11th June 1868, the church was solemnly inaugurated and given the name of Our Lady of Victories.[87] "*It was a Feast day for all the French Catholics... People from every district and suburb came together in Leicester Square. Mgr. Manning was seated on the left of the altar under a red canopy. Opposite him was the Pope's chamberlain. Then, about thirty ecclesiastics formed an impressive retinue. The Discalced Carmelites had sent two priests, the Little Sisters of the Poor came from Hammersmith and the St. Vincent de Paul Sisters (wearing their distinctive habits, now becoming rather popular in London) arrived with the orphans entrusted to their care, completing the procession.*

The entrance to the church was through a porch in Leicester Place. Four galleries, raised to a certain height, provided more space for an increased number of faithful. On the right was the altar of the Blessed Virgin Mary and on the left St. Joseph's altar. There was a huge crowd standing outside throughout the ceremony. The tireless Father Faure was there, as always busy supervising his workers, never leaving them except to find money to pay them. He gave a blessing with the Blessed Sacrament. The church just had to be finished and there still remained so much to do".[88]

THE FIRST CHURCH 1865-1940

"The church was arched with a cast-iron framework like St. Eugene's Church in Paris.[89] The space in between the metal ridges was filled with cement. Because the building was surrounded by other constructions it wasn't possible to have more than two stained-glass rose windows.[90] Openings made in the roof gave light to the whole building. The machinery for heating and ventilation was in the basement. The main altar was an elegant construction in terracotta, created by Viribert from Toulouse. The tabernacle, canopy and crucifix were all in richly gilded metal. Both side altars, consecrated to Our Lady and St. Joseph were very ornate."[91]

To furnish the new sanctuary, the Arch-confraternity of Our Lady of Victories offered the altar of the Virgin and a marble statue of Our Lady of Victories, a replica of the one in Paris. "Before sending it to London it was kept one night in the Parisian sanctuary so as to communicate its supernatural virtue..."[92] The statue of Mary above the altar consecrated to her, was a gift from the Church of St. Sulpice in Paris and the pulpit was donated by the princely Orleans family.

Shortly after the inauguration Father Faure arranged to have a large marble plaque on display in Notre Dame de Victoires Church in Paris with the inscription: *We acknowledge and pay homage to you Our Lady of Victories, Mother and Foundress of Notre Dame de France in London. Protect and guide us always! May Jesus, Mary and Joseph reign there as they do here! 8th December 1868.*

The organ in Notre Dame de France was inaugurated on the 18th March 1868. It was built by Auguste Gern, former director of the workshops of the celebrated Parisian organ builder Aristide Cavaillé-Coll.[93] Gern came to London to build several instruments before he set up his own company there in 1866. He made his first organ for Notre Dame de France.[94]

Whilst the old Panorama had its entrance at 16 Leicester Square Boileau changed the entrance for the church to 5 Leicester Place. The ground floor formed a passage giving access to the church. Above this, on the first floor, there was a library, a parlour and a dining room. Father Faure occupied the second floor, his curate the third, and the housekeeper the fourth. The kitchen was in the basement. A staircase joined the various levels.

3. Establishing the Mission

This new French mission appeared just when the Catholic faith in England entered a distinctive period of renewal. After the initial repeal of penal laws in 1791, Catholics were finally free to practise their religion again from 1829 onwards. Then in 1850 the Catholic hierarchy was re-established with Cardinal Wiseman being appointed as the first Archbishop of Westminster since the Anglican reformation. It was he who so diligently oversaw the establishment of Notre Dame de France. A number of spectacular conversions followed these developments – for example, John Henry Newman,[95] a future cardinal, and Henry Manning[96] who was the successor of Cardinal Wiseman as Archbishop of Westminster. Manning was just as determined as Wiseman to help the new French parish.

The French Catholic clergy who emigrated at the end of the 18th century gained the respect and esteem of everyone because of their worthy demeanour and compassion. They were responsible for the foundation of many chapels which, after they returned to France, became very active English Catholic parishes. The influence of the French Catholics possibly accelerated the restoration of the Catholic religion in England. It benefitted from the French model of Church across the Channel in many ways: in architecture and in the neo-Gothic style of decorating churches which was dear to Viollet-le-Duc;[97] in certain aspects of liturgy;[98] and in the choice of devotions to the Sacred Heart, to Saint Therese of the Child Jesus and to Our Lady of Lourdes.

At the beginning of 1866 a second Marist, Father Léon Thomas, came to help Father Faure. Father Faure had also invited three Sisters of St. Vincent de Paul. The latter soon opened a crèche, a girls' school[99] in Leicester Place and a boys' school in the house[100] which adjoined the Rotunda and was included in the lease. The boys' school was scarcely opened when it reached an enrolment of 80 pupils. In 1890 this school would be transferred to an adjacent house in Lisle Street. A small hospital of 16 beds, entrusted to the Sisters, was opened in 1867 at the corner of Leicester Place and Lisle Street. It merged with the Dispensary[101] under the name of *The French Hospital and Dispensary*. During the first year, 300 patients were admitted and nearly 8,000 outpatients were given treatment there by the Sisters of St. Vincent de Paul with religious assistance provided by the Marist Fathers.

Catholic Embassy Chapels

The prohibition of the Catholic religion in England since the Anglican Reformation obliged the ambassadors of the King of France and the other Catholic powers who were endowed with extraterritorial privileges over their establishments, to maintain their own chapels. There were many such Catholic chapels in London attached to the embassies of Spain, Portugal, Sicily, Sardinia, Bavaria, not forgetting Venice.

French Catholics in transit, such as merchants and travellers, had access to the French chapel. Beside the ambassador and his family the English who remained Catholic, despite the persecutions, were also welcome. This arrangement lasted until the end of the 18th century. The fate of the French chapel followed that of the embassy. Both had to move house whenever hostilities flared up between the two countries. So, between the 17th and 18th centuries the French embassy and its chapel changed location a dozen times.

As the activities expanded the challenges multiplied. So considerable was the work carried out for the French community in Leicester Square that Notre Dame de France was always in need of new resources. Fundraising events, some quite brilliant, were simply not enough. The struggling parish, having borrowed to start, had to find 20,000 francs annually just to survive!

From August 1870 onwards a fresh wave of refugees arrived, fleeing from the Prussians, increasing the French population of Soho. They were followed closely by the *communards* pursued by the Thiers government in France.

By 1872 every Sunday saw 700-800 people coming to church. An annual directory of the parish gives more details: during the winter of 1874 poor children received 7,440 meals and 3,600 bowls of soup; Notre Dame de France paid the rent for 450 impoverished families and delivered 7 tons of coal; jobs were provided for the women, especially in the workshops where they made artificial flowers.

The schools for the boys and the girls, the crèche and the orphanage constituted a heavy burden on the Sisters of St. Vincent de Paul. In 1870 the orphanage was transferred to Norwood in South London. In 1878, the Sisters of St. Vincent de Paul had to be replaced by the Servant Sisters of the Sacred Heart. A few years later, the Sisters of the Blessed Sacrament took over. The boys' school, having been opened and closed several times in the course of the early years, was finally entrusted to the care of the Marist Brothers in 1892. The hospital was extended in 1878 and transferred to a building in Shaftsbury Avenue in 1890.[103]

Obtaining ownership of the site of the church and its annexes[104] was always Father Faure's major concern.[105] The *freehold*[106] ownership was negotiated by him, authorised by Cardinal Manning and finally bought by the Society of Mary in 1899.

With the project now firmly established, the aim of the mission was realised – namely, to provide assistance in education, charitable works, and religion for the French immigrants. Charles Faure left London for good in 1881.

4. An Expanding Mission

Between the departure of Father Faure and the beginning of the First World War, nine Marist Fathers[107] succeeded each other as superiors of Notre Dame de France. Six of them lasted from one to five years whilst three renewed their ministry. The archives of the church mention two of them in particular.

The first, Father Jean Thomas, was *"an orderly man who devoted his time to organising the work better".*[108] He was given the opportunity to prove it during a requiem mass in Notre Dame de France on the 2nd July 1894, after the assassination of President Sadi Carnot. *"The church was richly decorated for the occasion. Black drapes fringed with gold hung gracefully from the top of the vault right down along the sides of the church, the columns were entwined with giant palms emerging from beds of flowers around each base, escutcheons, innumerable lights, flags and finally, a rich catafalque sparkling with gold, completed the decoration. The presence of very many uniformed military created an aura of splendour."*[109] *"Never since the Reformation was there such a dazzling attendance in a Catholic church in England."*[110]

The second, Father Jean-Baptiste Gay, was known as *"a man of the ordinary people. He went around all the kitchens in London to visit his parishioners."*[111] He was responsible for further major renovations. In 1903 the access to the church needed to be enlarged without delay and in 1911 the whole interior had to be renovated. That same year a vast circular terrace, made from reinforced brick, was constructed on the top of the building.

In 1909, the year when Joan of Arc was beatified, Father Gay officially instituted her feast day. *"The feast was celebrated with the support of the French authorities and of the cadets from the Society of Military Training (Société de Préparation Militaire) gathered around the tricolour flag".*[112] *"Dressed with helmet, breastplate and steel boots a young girl from the parish took the place of the Lorraine heroine."*[113] In 1911, he celebrated the first midnight mass in Notre Dame de France.

Father Gay had not been long the superior when he received a visit in 1905 from the French Ambassador, Paul Cambon, just after France had voted for the separation[114] of Church and State. *"Paul Cambon*[115] *asked him that, officially as from that day, it was to be the French Embassy church and to place two reserved pews in the church- one for the Ambassador and the other for the Consul General of France."*[116] He proved to be one of the most important figures of the French community during his long mission as Ambassador, being the person behind the *Entente Cordiale* between France and England.[117] He was in London when war was declared against Germany in August 1914. Father Maxime Robin was Rector of the parish. Father Robin was *"one of the most popular figures of Notre Dame de France at the beginning of the 20th century. As a priest he personified goodness. He gave all that he had."*[118]

While the hostilities lasted a number of women, members of the Red Cross, used to stand outside the door of the church and collect the offerings given for the relief of the French wounded in battle. The parish was associated with "*the Committee assisting families of French soldiers fighting under the flag*". It would keep in storage the furniture of many families in the basement of the church and the nearby houses.

The influx of Belgian refugees to England at this time brought with it some permanent changes. Suddenly Notre Dame de France had to cater for all French-speaking Catholics regardless of their nationality. Ever since then such hospitality has characterized Notre Dame de France.

A school was opened near Victoria Station in 1915 for the children of Belgian refugees. It had 120 pupils. The name *Lycée Français* appears for the first time in 1920 when it was installed in South Kensington, opposite the Victoria and Albert Museum. There were between 300 and 400 students.[119] From the very beginning the Marist Fathers were the chaplains.

In the first third of the century the French community was transformed. It became very prosperous and distanced itself from Soho. It settled in the South-West, especially in the quarters of Kensington and Chelsea.[120]

At that time the parish schools[121] and the crèche counted around 250 children. On the 31st December 1921, the parish registers mentioned 2,053 marriages and 6,819 baptisms of infants and adults celebrated since the beginning of the mission.

36   CHAPTER II

Soon Notre Dame de France initiated other works. Activities geared more towards youth were added to the ministries of social outreach and education that had been prominent in the initial fifty years. Between 1928 and 1930 the first troop of Scouts was formed from all denominations at the Lycée. Very soon there were 4 *patrols* and a *pack* attached to the Scouts of France.[122] In 1930 the scouts from the French Lycée participated in its first grand cultural event, the Birkenhead *Jamboree*.

Notre Dame de France also developed the reputation for being a church which welcomed priests and bishops in transit. Ordinarily there were two low masses on weekdays but sometimes there were as many as ten. Parishioners of that time remembered that in 1908, during the international Eucharistic Congress, up to forty masses were celebrated daily. As many priests again attended those masses because of the impossibility of themselves celebrating.

In 1938-39 a new electrical heating system was installed in the church and the interior was completely renovated. At the same time the firm J.W. Walker & Sons Ltd. rebuilt and enlarged the organ.

A year later France went to war against Nazi Germany.

5. The Second World War

On the 18th June 1940 the call issued by General de Gaulle in London gave birth to Free France. Father Francois Laurent,[123] a 64 year old Belgian who had been one of the pioneers of the Marist Mission in the Solomon Islands, was then superior in Notre Dame de France. He had been superior since 1933.

At that time, "*the French community in London numbered approximately 10,000... merchants, cooks, business men, garage owners. They lived in Soho, South Kensington, Clapham, Richmond, and Wimbledon. Their young children attended the parish school in Notre Dame de France...*"[124]

The welcome given by the French to General de Gaulle was mixed. Some among the more well-known figures returned to France or left for the United States.[125] Others stayed on, encouraged by the creation of the association *French of Great Britain*, which helped to gather together those men and women who gave their support to Free France.

The Free French Forces

The troops who had embarked at Dunkirk and the survivors from the Narvik campaign streamed into England. The majority of the French military returned to France. A small number rallied around General de Gaulle. Others would follow – soldiers, sailors, airmen – who arrived from France, either individually or in convoys.

By the end of July 1940 around 7,000 had joined up with General de Gaulle who had established himself in No. 4 Carlton Gardens. The students from the French Lycée in South Kensington had been evacuated to the Lake District in the North of England and their building became the Headquarters of the Free French Air Force.

Civilians of every political colour and every social level also joined up – republicans, socialists, communists, practising Catholics, intellectuals, scientists, sailors, students... All felt strongly motivated and wanted to fight. Some, who were still adolescents, falsified their papers to hide their age and took considerable risks to get to England.

Women also joined the Free French. After November 1940, they became members of the *Women Volunteers of Free France* and were organised according to the model of the women's auxiliaries of the British army.

For recreation, the French officers would get together at the *Petit Club* in St. James' Square where they could drink late into the night and dance to the music of French songs. The younger French went to pubs, jazz clubs, cinemas, and to less well-regarded cabarets in Soho, which the residents referred to as "*their village*": "*...All the people knew each other and were on speaking terms. When I was twelve I used to do deliveries for my mother (a milliner) and I would meet up with the Free French, all of them so young... I attended school at the Sisters in Notre Dame de France... they would ask us to invite them to our parents' homes...*"[126]

Since the armistice in June 1940 England had been left all alone against Nazi Germany which wanted to force her to seek peace. To this end the Blitz or the bombing of London began on the 7th September 1940 and lasted until the 27th May 1941,[127] killing almost 40,000 people and leaving 1.5 million homeless. For nearly nine months from nightfall until dawn the German bombers, refuelling at Cap Gris airbase, invaded the London skies: "*Search lights ripped the London night apart. Towards midnight the ground trembled and we heard the noise of broken glass, the gunfire of the DCA, and the rumbling of the Nazi planes bombarding the docks... The head lights of the cars only let through a thin shaft of light... As soon as the sirens sounded the pedestrians hurried to the basements... At night, people slept in the Underground... At dawn, following the alerts, the street smelt of smoke, diesel and explosives. Pieces of shrapnel littered the ground around the ruins.*"[128]

In his diary Father Laurent wrote about the alerts for these air raids: "*I no longer ring the rising bell at 4.30 a.m. as there are three, five or seven alerts every 24 hours.*" (14 September) "*I slept well enough under the altar, Father Robin and Father de Silva slept in the confessional, Father Perrot in the library and Father Dumas in his own room.*"

On the 6th November 1940 the 308th air raid alert was given. Father Laurent's commentary was very brief: "*At 8.20,*[129] *two bombs hit the church in front of the main altar. The Fathers are safe. At 9.20, we sought refuge in the hospital.*"

A parishioner gave more details: "*This Wednesday evening the sirens announced that foreign planes in formation had crossed the English coast. [The Fathers] dined around seven in the evening before going down to the crypt which was used as a shelter. There, under the main altar, they kept a radio intended to keep them company whenever the excessively violent bombing forced them, like everyone else, down to the basements. At eight o'clock the BBC would broadcast the news and it was the custom for the Fathers to go down to the crypt to listen in. That particular evening, either the radio or the electricity didn't work... so our Fathers, deprived of their companion in the shelter, went back up to their rooms situated around the church.*

Very shortly afterwards a series of two or three bombs made a direct hit on the roof of the church, smashed through it, each bomb making a hole, and then landed at the foot of the main altar but went through the floor and exploded right where the Fathers usually took shelter. The crypt and the church were just a heap of rubble, broken planks and twisted beams making it difficult to walk through. As for the Fathers, they were spared and their rooms as well, and the fact that they didn't die was due to the silence of the radio..."[130]

Father Laurent's diary then tells what happened next: "*At 10 o'clock we found the Blessed Sacrament in the debris. I carried it to the hospital. The sailors from the French Merchant Navy helped us to clear up the rubble... While searching through the ruins the following morning, a worker discovered the ciborium wrapped in a piece of the altar cloth. The hosts were inside, intact...* [in the church] *all that remained were the tabernacle from a side-altar and a few statues...*"[131]

The outer brick walls of the old Panorama, although sixty centimetres thick, were broken in many places. Thanks to its round shape the effect of the explosion did not achieve maximum impact. Some statues even remained undamaged. The floor and the ceilings were destroyed but architect Boileau's iron framework survived rather well. Three of the four pillars were practically intact. In among the ruins the statue of Our Lady of Victories was found in pieces: "*Of (the Virgin) whose face expressed ineffable gentleness, only the head remained, marked with splinters...*"[132]

It was unthinkable to close the church in a time of war. Even in a damaged state it had to continue to serve. A chapel was improvised in the nearby school but "*The safety department hesitated to allow it to be used in case the walls would collapse... On the first Sunday without a church it was in this chapel that the masses were celebrated and the usual choirs, accompanied by a grand piano, were led by our organist, M. Page.*"[133]

The building needed major repairs but labour was scarce, materials limited and administrative procedures made it difficult to get permission to rebuild or, in this case, to repair it. The determination of Father Laurent allied to the competence of the architects, Stanley Hall & Eason and Roberson, overcame all obstacles. As soon as the licence was issued in March 1941 rebuilding began. The architects worked wonders in order to save what remained: pillars were propped up, holes in the walls were filled in and the iron framework was enclosed in a strong casing. Meanwhile the organ was dismantled by the firm J.W. Walker & Sons and stored in a warehouse to keep it safe.

On the 7th July the Provincial of Paris received this telegram: "*Workers restore ruins of church. Hoping to be back in there before Christmas. 300 people in the temporary chapel every Sunday. Schools escape intact. Let us keep up our courage as Marists do. – Robin*". Exactly eight months later, on the 2nd November, the church was reopened "*after many important repairs had been carried out*", as the press reported.

At that time, the presbytery was in just as pitiful state as the church. Already before the war, the rooms needed refurbishing. With the bombings "*the house became a slum*".[134] The war and the bombings also had disastrous effects on the health of the Marists: in January 1941 Father Perrot died from a massive heart attack; in April Father Laurent was hospitalised for seven weeks and in August Father Robin was also hospitalised.

As time went on the provisional restoration work deteriorated little by little. Sometimes one could see fragments of the collapsed wall in the church. In spite of this the parish records mention that births and the numbers of marriages registered were as many as in peace time! "*Fathers de Silva, van Offen and van der Lucht are here. As soon as possible we must put back some French blood in the team. It is both necessary and urgent. We are not suffering from rationing but the French colony in London is much reduced. We have, however, enough to do. Outside work is not lacking if I had the personnel – retreats, confessions in convents…*"[135]

Correspondence addressed to the Provincial of Paris between 1941-45 indicated that "*…the work of the mission continues … although reduced by the force of circumstances. Our schools remain open.*[136] *We have a Marist Brother for English and our sacristan teaches French… We have only 60 children instead of 180 as in normal times. For twelve months we said Mass in a classroom in the girls' school. Now, thanks be to God, we are back in our church although patched up and reduced.*"[137]

THE FIRST CHURCH 1865-1940   41

So it was that even in its darkest days during the war Notre Dame de France church was never closed and the Fathers did their best to give spiritual help and comfort to their parishioners. Just like the shopkeepers who cleared away the pieces of shrapnel and the debris of glass in front of their shops each morning and put up the signs "*business as usual*", so also the Marist Fathers of Notre Dame de France did not cease to live and work in their church. They continued their activities in the neighbourhood welcoming the soldiers, officers and French civilians who came to swell the ranks of the parishioners of every age.

THE FIRST CHURCH 1865-1940

CHAPTER III

III. The Second Church: Reconstruction

1. The End of the War and the Reconstruction

Volunteers re-joining the Free French continued to arrive in London until General de Gaulle left for Algiers in May 1943. Some became regular visitors to Notre Dame de France. One such visitor was Maurice Schumann[138] – a convert to Catholicism in 1937. Another was Colonel Rémy, founder of the information network *Confraternity of Notre Dame*.

Colonel Rémy was a fervent Catholic, particularly attached to Marian devotion saying *"I must see Notre Dame de France Church again in March 1942, in between two missions... Of the statue (Our Lady of Victories) before which I prayed only the head remains... Father Rector entrusted it to me"*.[139] When Colonel Rémy returned to France (by parachute!) after the invasion of the allied forces landed in France he took with him the head from the statue of the Virgin destroyed in the bombing. From this a duplicate of the statue was made. He wrote

Colonel Rémy

the following in his *Memoirs*: *"Mr. Henry Valette,[140] a Parisian sculptor, took on the task. When Paris was liberated my first visit was to him. More than two metres high and cut in stone, Our Lady seemed to be waiting for me. To transport the statue to England it had to be divided into three sections... I persuaded the captain of the mail boat which sailed between Dieppe and New Haven to take it on board although I didn't have any authorisation...[141] On seeing the three cases offloaded in the English port I breathed a sigh of relief... The plaque, now lost, which accompanied it had this inscription: As a tribute of gratitude from the survivors of the Confraternity of Notre Dame network in the occupied zone... (On the 27th January 1946) The inauguration, which I dreamed of for three years, took place in the presence of the Bishop of Westminster (sic)[142] Still ravaged and supported by props the nave of the church threatened to collapse with so many people crammed into it. The good Rector[143] was bursting with joy... Dear friends... There is happiness in the air... after four years Our Lady of Victories has returned to her niche. You know how good the Blessed Virgin is and how she doesn't refuse anything to her children... on a day like this all of us are sure to be heard. Come on, don't hesitate. As for me, I am going to spell out the requests of the parish. Opening the exercise book which he had in his hand, he read aloud: Three young people and their future, a family looking for a flat. And the conversion of England. Amen."*[144]

It was difficult to find a place for the statue because of its size so it was eventually installed in the balcony of the new church.[145] The original head from the statute of the Virgin which Colonel Rémy had carried with him back to France was finally sealed on his tomb.

Meanwhile, after the bombing of the church and into the beginning of the 1950s, when there were less than 10,000 French in London, the Marists continued to do their best to meet the pastoral needs of their parishioners, whether they were French or English. There was a great need to always have a priest available for confessions in the church: *"People came from all corners of London – priests, religious and faithful. Seven out of ten confessions were in English!"*[146] The Marists also supplied chaplains for the hospital and the Lycée and supported the Marist Sisters in London – *"A better life gets under way and we can never forget those to whom we owe this rebirth, in particular Frs Deguerry, Jacquemin and Le Creurer..."*[147]

Notre Dame de France had survived the war but it was clear that a new church was needed. The hastily improvised repair work done after the bombing was only provisional. The difficulties then encountered in obtaining building materials had compromised the work: *"The timber available wasn't enough, so in order to find enough space, we had to change the position of the altar and use second-hand planks treated with creosote."*[148] It would have been better to rebuild the church entirely but it was almost unthinkable at this time of severe restrictions: *"Not only* [must we] *convince the French and British authorities of our willingness to revive* [Notre Dame de France] *but also ensure that we have the necessary finance. The proposal also needs to be acceptable, i.e. the architectural plans must be suitable, with a choice of quality materials and some works of contemporary religious art as decoration."*[149]

René Varin and Marist Fathers

At a time when England was focussed only on building homes an exceptional license to rebuild the church was required. In 1952 the licence to rebuild was granted through the intervention of

Anthony Eden,[150] who was the English Minister of Foreign Affairs and on friendly terms with the French Ambassador René Massigli.[151] Father Francisque Deguerry the new superior since September 1948,[152] resisted the suggestion to leave Leicester Place and move closer to the French community which had moved towards the west of the city. To do so may well have been logical but it would not have been faithful to the purpose of the Marist mission in London. For the same reason he declined the offer of a theatre company which proposed to build at their expense in the suburbs of London a new church with a presbytery and an ultra-modern school in exchange for the site of the old Panorama.

Father Deguerry was determined to rebuild the church on its original site: "*Courage, we have the site... money will come*" he promised his parishioners. In a hurry to get back "their" church the parishioners were very generous organising many fundraising events, sales and bazaars to raise money. They were helped by the Rebuilding Committee which was supervised by Pierre Dormeuil, President of the French Chamber of Commerce in London.

Nothing would have been possible without the active participation of two of the French authorities in London: Jean Chauvel, Ambassador from 1955 until 1962, and especially René Varin,[153] Cultural Attaché to the Embassy for fourteen years, the man responsible for the restoration of Versailles Castle and a friend of André Malraux. It was Varin who recommended the architect, Hector Corfiato,[154] a British citizen but of Greek descent and a former student of the School of Fine Arts (*École des Beaux-Arts*) in Paris. But Corfiato was forced to implement the wishes of John-Charles Moreux,[155] another *Beaux-Arts* Architect, who supervised the construction from Paris. Moreux insisted upon his design which included following the classical tradition of having twelve pillars.

A London contractor, C.P. Roberts, was chosen to carry out Corfiato's plans. The estimated cost rose to £200,000. The allocation for war damages covered £110,000, the gifts and subscriptions of the parishioners £29,000 while the Congregation of the Marists promised £50,000.

Work started in January 1953. The architect's task was delicate. The circular form, inherited from the former Panorama, had to preserve the French influence of the first church whilst incorporating a more modern style. The result was a light, ordered, "Cartesian"

church. A more difficult and audacious design of Corfiato was abandoned, doubtless because of the costs involved.

Maurice Schumann, an early member of the Gaullist cause in London, now the Secretary of State for Foreign Affairs – laid the first stone of the new building on the 31st May 1953 in the presence of Marshal Juin. He had come to London for the coronation of Queen Elizabeth. The stone was taken from amongst the oldest stones of Notre Dame de Chartres and was a gift from the administration of the Historical Monuments of Paris. The inscription on the stone reads: *Notre Dame de Chartres 1194-1260, Notre Dame de France 1865-1953*.

In order to use the full potential of the site, the architect had the builders dig under the church and convert this area into a large space designed for parish events: conferences, concerts, films, theatre, sales. This space, inaugurated on the 11th May 1954, served as a place of worship until the official opening of the church eighteen months later.

The church of Notre Dame de France was reopened for worship on the 6th October 1955 and solemnly inaugurated by the Archbishops of Paris[156] and of Westminster[157] in the presence of the official representatives of the French community: *"This was a praiseworthy achievement... for the Marist Fathers... and for the numerous members of the faithful who contributed to the work by their generous gifts... Those responsible, however, had to borrow 25 million francs through a French bank... To repay this loan they are counting on hiring out the splendid parish hall"*.

Accessible from the street, at the top of several steps, there was a vestibule leading into the new church which occupied the circular space of the old Panorama: *"A colonnade forms a circular gallery which allows one to go around of the church, forming a sacristy behind the altar. In addition, there is a first floor terraced balcony furnished with pews which doubles the number of available places. The five storey presbytery is built between the church and the street opening out on to a terrace built on the roof."*[158]

"It is an extremely sober construction... Thanks to a small dome which has an openwork design the main altar shows up very clearly... No candelabra. The walls, which are still awaiting the Stations of the Cross, are white like the steps in the sanctuary. Lighting is indirect. The two chairs at the side of the walls, the monolith of the main altar and the pillars on which it rests are also of white stone from Portland. Panelling is rare and discreet. There is some in the circular gallery and in the two confessionals... three wrought iron doors give access to the porch [vestibule]. The [concave façade] of yellow brick is adorned with a group [of sculptures] several metres in height..."[160]

48   CHAPTER III

In the same year the firm J.W. Walker & Sons installed a new organ which retained very little of the instrument made by Gern in 1868.

Father Deguerry had fought hard for the church to be rebuilt on the original site but he would not see it finished as he died suddenly in May 1953. He was succeeded by Father Paul Jacquemin. He directed the remaining construction work and decoration of the church. Father Jacquemin also oversaw the post war development of the mission of Notre Dame de France.

2. The Decoration of the New Church

Sacred Art and the Second World War

The decoration of the new church was started and completed at a time when church art was being heavily influenced by the ideas of Father Couturier.[161] He belonged to a movement – born after the First World War and strengthened after the Second World War – which set as its goal the renewal of religious art in Catholic churches. This movement deliberately sought to break away from academicism and Saint Sulpician sentimentality. Father Couturier encouraged the commissioning of major works for churches from avant-garde artists, whether they were Christian or not:[162] *"All true art is sacred. It is better to engage men of genius who have no faith than believers who lack talent."* Father Couturier declared.

As cultural attaché at the French Embassy, René Varin took it upon himself to ensure that Notre Dame de France would be a lasting monument to the finest of contemporary French art. Besides recommending Corfiato to be the architect he also chose the artists who would decorate the church.

THE SECOND CHURCH: RECONSTRUCTION   49

2.1. The Notre-Dame-de-France Tapestry of Dom Robert

When the reconstructed church was inaugurated on the 16th October 1955, a large tapestry[163] was displayed above the main altar. It had just been completed in the workshops of Aubusson according to the drawing of Dom Robert OSB.

Dom Robert – monk, theologian and artist who loved nature – was born Guy de Chaunac-Lanzac. He was a member of the Benedictine monastery of En Calcat in Tarn, and a pupil and friend of Jean Lurcat.[164] Fleeing from the bustle of a fashionable artist's career, which did not fit in with the Benedictine rule, Dom Robert retired from 1948 until 1957 to the Benedictine Abbey of Buckfast in Devon, England. It was there that he designed the model in poster paint for the future tapestry in Notre Dame de France. Dom Robert described this process of "colouring", saying: "*My sketches are generally numbered, that is to say that each zone of colours is indicated by a number... Each colour is subdivided into many nuanced shades from clear to dark and numbered in order. In all there are 40 shades of eight basic colours. A numbered cartoon requires ...a more sensitive and more exact style of drawing... avoiding especially any flabbiness of form. Above all one avoids the risk of the tapestry being a simple copy of the painting.*"[165]

The artistic language of Dom Robert is made up almost exclusively of flowers, herbs and abstract motifs, inspired by nature. Sometimes a few animals are included. First in his watercolours and then in his tapestry sketches he brings back to life the ancient tradition of "*millefiori*" or "*verdures*", a type of wall-hanging mostly decorated with floral motifs which was highly prized in the 15th and 16th centuries. Dom Robert used a collection of familiar animals like those he might meet in the French or English countryside. However, they were not chosen by chance, as nearly all of them were Christ-like symbols, namely the lamb, the deer, the cock, the peacock, the phoenix, butterflies and fish. The squirrel belongs to the collection of animals associated with the Annunciation, while the goose is an image of vigilance and attachment to its Master.

The tapestry in Notre Dame de France is Dom Robert's biggest tapestry and one of the rare ones depicting a human figure. On a background of azure blue,[166] bordered with red edging, a young woman appears in a white dress, wearing a light veil and a large halo around her head. This gives the scene a sacred character while the colour of her dress is a symbol of purity. The figure is standing on a sort of little island in the middle of verdant scenery and surrounded by all kinds of animals. The border and the motifs along the four sides, as well as the Latin quotation at the bottom of the work, are reminders that Dom Robert started his apprenticeship as an artist in En Calcat, painting illuminations for a Gospel book. In the monastic tradition for illuminations both text and image are associated with each other and sometimes there is the added presence of one or several characters.

There is a more theological explanation for this young woman placed in a setting of earthly paradise. She symbolises Wisdom. The quotation in Latin is an excerpt from the Book of Proverbs and refers to Wisdom, present at God's side at the time when the world was created: "*Cum eo eram cuncta componens* Ludens coram eo omni tempore*" Proverbs 8,30 ("I was by his side, like a master craftsman, ever at play in his presence.") The liturgy applies this text also to the Virgin Mary whom the early Fathers of the Church quickly named the New Eve. The title of the tapestry, according to the Abbot of En Calcat, is indeed The New Eve.

The tapestry was ordered by the French Embassy for Notre Dame de France, following the advice of René Varin. Since the French state commissioned the work and financed its purchase the tapestry remains the property of the State.

2.2 The Virgin of Mercy Bas-relief by Georges Saupique

René Varin also succeeded in gaining the collaboration of George Saupique,[167] a French sculptor, well known as head of the statuary restoration team in Rheims Cathedral. He came to London in 1953 to finish "in situ" the Virgin of Mercy made of Bourgogne stone, roughed out beforehand by his assistant and placed above the entrance to Notre Dame de France. With a halo round her head, Mary is standing very still and facing outwards. With outstretched hands she is opening the folds of her cloak within which are a crowd of people, symbolically much smaller than herself, some standing and others kneeling. She bows her head towards the Infant Jesus who

appears as Christ the Saviour of the world. He is holding in his left hand the world and giving a blessing with his right. All this is contained in a mandorla,[168] an almond shaped piece of art, indicating a sacred person. Jesus is "seated" on his mother's breast who is displaying the characteristics of the Virgin who holds the one whom the Universe cannot hold, God himself. In iconography this image of the Virgin is called the "Platytera"[169] Virgin – the Virgin who is more spacious than the heavens.

Positioned as she is, visible from the street, the Virgin can be understood either as the Church welcoming humanity or the Church receiving not only the parishioners who are about to enter the building but anyone at all who may wish to do so.

The two columns of the porch are decorated with eight bands, sculptured in bas-relief, representing different episodes in the life of the Virgin Mary. Some of them signed the bas-reliefs are the work of Georges Saupique's students at the School of Fine Arts (*École des Beaux-Arts*). The same students made for Notre Dame de France a wooden statue of St. Joseph which is placed inside the church.

2.3. The Baptismal Font and the Ambos

The baptismal font, decorated in bas-relief, was cut in sandstone from the Vosges in 1954 by the Notre Dame de Strasbourg workshops under the direction of Emile Stoll,[170] a sculptor from Alsace. On the upper half each sacrament is represented by a symbol. On the lower half each is illustrated by a scene from the Gospel.

A sculptor from the School of Fine Arts (*École des Beaux-Arts*)[171] came from Paris, again at the request of René Varin, to engrave two blocks of stone cut by the students from the school. These blocks became the ambos, the two lecterns from which the readings are traditionally proclaimed. The silhouettes of the prophets Isaiah, Jeremiah, Ezekiel and Daniel are engraved on the one on the right and the symbols of the four Evangelists – a Man, a Lion, an Ox and an Eagle – are on the one on the left.

2.4. The Mosaic of the Nativity by Boris Anrep

In the side chapel consecrated to Mary, the front of the altar was decorated in 1954 with a mosaic by Boris Anrep,[172] a Russian artist who came to England after the 1917 revolution. He became famous for his mosaic floor at the Tate Gallery in 1923, inspired by the Proverbs of William Blake, and, ten years later by another vast mosaic floor at the entrance of the National Gallery, representing an allegorical cycle in which the characters have the faces of celebrities and artists of the time. Amongst other work Anrep decorated the Blessed Sacrament Chapel in Westminster Cathedral, the head office of the Bank of England and many private residences.

The subject of the mosaic in Notre Dame de France is the Nativity. Dominating the scene is the figure of the Virgin kneeling down, tenderly bending over the infant Jesus in the crib. We see on the right the traditional donkey and ox and on the left the star of Bethlehem: "*As the colouring of the church is of a delicate brightness and whitish, the major effect of colour is reserved for the tapestry* [of Dom Robert] *displayed behind the main altar... I tried my best to find a series of discreet colours which are harmonious and, at the same time, expressive. As a base I used the Portland stone from which the altar is made and took highly coloured Venetian enamel solely for the contours of the characters involved... The forms become less opaque, their transparency makes the image ethereal, freed from all that is mateerial... a quality which is of the utmost importance in religious art.*"[173]

When painting the walls of the chapel in November 1959, Jean Cocteau, as a widely admired artist, decided to conceal Anrep's mosaic behind a wooden panel decorated by him with a large M,[174] thus extending one of the motifs of the Crucifixion scene. The panel was removed and hung on a wall outside the chapel when the church was refurbished in 2004. The mosaic has since been cleaned and is now clearly visible in the place for which it had been created.

2.5. Preparations and Painting of the Murals by Jean Cocteau

Up to 1958 the walls of the only side chapel, where the Blessed Sacrament was reserved,[175] were decorated with prints of French Cathedrals and an inscription: "Love Mary and make her loved". On the left of the altar there was a copy in wood of a 14th century Virgin from the Isle of France carved by an unknown teacher at the School of Boulle.[176]

To decorate the walls of the chapel with an original work, René Varin appealed to a friend to whom he had recently done a favour:[177] "*I called on... Cocteau, because I thought we should include some contemporary art, as long as it was not outrageous.*[178] *Cocteau is a man... full of fantasy, full of fun... but keeping in his deepest heart and thoughts, a certain number of areas which he shares with no one, his private domain. Faith is one of these areas which he enters alone.*"[179]

Right from the beginning, Father Yves Le Creurer followed the plan for the decoration of the chapel: "*René Varin put it to us[180] one day in 1956: I had occasion to visit Jean Cocteau... He was finishing the decoration of the Fishermen's Chapel in Villefranche... I asked him if he would accept to provide frescos in the same style for our French church in London. He immediately agreed to do so.*"[181]

The plan did not take shape until 1959, delayed by Jean Cocteau's multiple artistic, literary and cinematic engagements. After having turned down the initial offer to paint the vestibule of Notre Dame de France of which he had seen a model -"*There are many doors, it is only a passageway.*"- Cocteau accepted to work in the Lady chapel, "*a little jewel*" he said.

The priests of Notre Dame de France, the Society of Mary in Paris and the artist came together to find the best subject: "*The theme which seemed essential for a church dedicated to Our Lady of Victories was the Virgin Mary. Leave it to the artist to express himself in his own style.*"[182]

Cocteau first of all sketched the Crucifixion. The priests were pleased with the theme but they thought the masculine characters were too sensual. The artist accepted to modify his sketches: "*All of a sudden... a telegram from Jean Cocteau in person: Give you my consent for the chapel, on my way. A few days later the diplomatic bag brought us the first sketches created by the artist for our chapel. It was in long rolls of transparent paper, upon which, when rolled out on the floor of our big dining room, three superb drawings appeared. They evoked, in grand stylised lines, the scenes of the Annunciation, the Crucifixion and the Assumption of the Virgin as we had suggested. While the overall work pleased, we all felt... rather hesitant in accepting some interpretations of the artist. Mr. Varin undertook once again to convey these concerns to Jean Cocteau...and a few weeks later we received a plan, reviewed and corrected according to our wishes.*"

In February, at the request of Cocteau, the walls were covered with a coating made mainly from sand and lime. Then Jean Triquenot, a painter from Nice, came in May to set up the sketches of the future drawings in charcoal.

At the beginning of November 1959 Cocteau was expected in London to make comments for the BBC on Stravinsky's Oedipus Rex[183] where he took up again his role in the choir. During that visit he would find a few days to do the work at Notre Dame de France. The media were intensely interested by Jean Cocteau's arrival in London where his films were enjoying great success. In particular television reporters and news photographers pressed so closely around him that it was necessary to build a wooden barrier around the chapel to protect the artist from the curious spectators. Father Jacquemin commented: "*We have avoided the Press so far. So, without any bother, it starts in peace and so in a Marist manner. I want this work to be strictly religious.*"[184]

Father Le Creurer hardly left Cocteau's side for a week: "*he spent a little more than eight days at his work...He arrived each morning around 10 am, dressed in a big grey cloak with a short cape, and the first thing he did was to stand before the statue of Our Lady of Lourdes,*[185] *light a candle and recollect himself for a few minutes before starting his work again... It was quite astonishing to hear him questioning his characters while he was working out the lines, colours and nuances. It was a real dialogue that he carried on with the wall of the chapel, using poetic words that seemed to spring from a sort of intense interior excitement. His joy was visible, especially when he was addressing the Virgin of the Annunciation... in a gripping face to face encounter from the top of his stepladder he would say to her: Oh you, the most beautiful of women, most beautiful of God's creatures, you are the most loved. I want you to be the most complete... When he stopped he would go and light candles, he used to light many candles...* "

Some days after his return to France, the artist wrote to the Marist Fathers: "*I am sad to leave, as if the wall of the chapel lured me into another world. I shall never forget that big open heart of Notre Dame de France and the place you have allowed me to take in it.*"[186]

THE SECOND CHURCH: RECONSTRUCTION   55

Description of the Murals

Created between the 3rd and the 11th November 1959 by Jean Cocteau, then sixty-one years of age, the murals take up three walls of the chapel and consist of three episodes of Mary's life: on the left the Annunciation, in the centre the Crucifixion and on the right the Assumption. The artist employed a classic technique for mural painting called "*a secco*". This is executed on a dry surface, unlike the technique called "*a fresco*" which is executed on a wet surface.

A. THE ANNUNCIATION

The scene is taken from the Gospel of Luke (1,26-28). The figure of the angel in the foreground is disproportionately large. There is a firm line extending to the vase[187] decorated with lilies, symbol of purity, before which the angel is bowing. He is dominates the tiny figure of Mary who is painted in the background with closed eyes and pale complexion. The words of the artist painting the scene revealed his own theological vision. "*On the day of the Annunciation, you are still an unfinished beauty. I draw the Angel with strong powerful lines for he is already real, the invisible made real, the only consisting reality. You, Mary, you hardly emerge in our misty world... I draw you in delicate lines. You are still the unfinished work of Grace...*"

Embellished with very few colours applied to the surface by rubbing dry paint brushes loaded with pigments, Cocteau's drawing is quite lineal. The style of the artist – drawings with lines almost without shadows – is easily identifiable and is situated somewhere in between drawing and writing.

B. THE CRUCIFIXION

The central scene in the chapel is unique in the depiction of crucifixions. It is the only one which shows just the legs and the feet of the crucified, the focal point of the painting. The black sun on the right recalls Mark's Gospel (14,33).

The characters are those described in the Crucifixion by the four Evangelists: Mary, the holy women, St John and the Roman soldiers who put Christ to death and played dice for his tunic. But the arrangement is unusual and the respective position of the characters is enigmatic. The women are united in their grief, by their intermingled veils which form the letter M, the initials of Mary and Magdalene. The one nearest to the onlooker, whose face is inclined towards the cross, is probably the mother of Jesus. She bows down before her dead son and accepts, with her hand on her heart, the will of God. Tears of blood fall from the eyes of the women to join with blood from the feet of the crucified, running down to the foot of the cross onto a big rose for which Cocteau has not given an explanation.[189]

His taste for the occult and for mystery, as much as his fleeting contact with a surrealistic group, find expression in his use of symbolic language, whether in his writing or painting, sometimes escaping interpretation.

In the foreground of this Crucifixion, the artist painted his own face but with his back to the scene. He has his eyebrow raised inquisitively. A falcon[190] is sitting beside his face. Is he hiding his own tears, or, is he turning away from the spectacle because he disowns it?

Taking up the same space as his self-portrait on the right of the painting is a character with an enigmatic expression. His eye, in the shape of a fish,[191] gives the impression that it might be Jesus, rising out of his bodily form, contemplating the scene of his death. Jean Cocteau, himself identified this character as Joseph of Arimathea.

C. THE ASSUMPTION

At the end of her life and accompanied by a choir of angels, the body and soul of Mary are taken up to heaven without experiencing death. The wrappings which traditionally cover the body of a corpse are undone and float in the air around her head, seat of the soul. They continue in a decorative wave which is characteristic of Cocteau's pictorial style.

The signature of the artist and the date are on the central panel of the Crucifixion preceded by the letters D.D.D: Jean Cocteau drew (Delineavit), consecrated (Dedicavit)

THE SECOND CHURCH: RECONSTRUCTION

and gave it as a gift (Donavit). It was indeed a gift because the artist refused any remuneration whatsoever, either for his work or for his stay in London. Cocteau returned to London for the inauguration of the paintings in May 1960. At his request the preparatory drawings were offered to Princess Margaret whom he had met.

The Cocteau chapel was cleaned and restored in 2012. Even if the works of art, which form an intrinsic part of the church, no longer conform to contemporary tastes in art, their quality enables them to transcend passing fashions and so they continue to attract visitors.

3. After the War: a New Lease of Life

Since the 1920s many changes had affected the French community, but Notre Dame de France was still their parish church: *"The French in London, much less numerous now, have moved from Soho towards Kensington and all the residential areas have become middle class (but) they do return to Soho and not only for amusement. They go there to pray, to have their children educated, for medical care when they are poor. The French Catholic community continued to live in Soho around their church, Notre Dame de France... Underneath its little white cross, the old entry with its grey door like so many others, sandwiched in between a hotel and a cinema, is rarely closed. During the week, in the midst of the Soho crowds, the one hundred and twenty children of the little French parish school pass through this door dressed in their school uniforms. All of Europe is represented on the benches of these small classrooms... In an office, a Marist Father is at the reception desk. He is the "welcoming Father". Many "passers-by" come to him, including those who live too far away to be here for Sunday... Five minutes' walk from there is the French hospital... open to all, the poor and sick whether French or those who speak French. The language doesn't matter much; what does matter is the poverty... That is what Notre Dame de France is all about. On Sunday mornings the French in London meet on the footpaths of Leicester Square, just like they would do after a village Mass... Some have a two hour journey to return to their homes in the residential suburbs."*[192]

After the war, all that remained in 16 Leicester Square was the girls' parish school which had reopened and was doing its best to survive. In July, the remaining 60 pupils occupied two rooms. The lessons were in English and a religious sister taught French for two hours each day. The boys' school closed in 1940 and did not reopen. The Marist Brothers had not returned and the municipality was opposed to reopening the establishment for reasons of health and safety.

Initially the director was Father Deguerry. When he died a hospital sister from the congregation of the Sisters of the Blessed Sacrament became the director. But the state of the school buildings and the teaching conditions for the sisters were deplorable. The rooms were badly lit and insufficiently ventilated. No financial help was given by the French government. When the directress was recalled by her superior the Marist Fathers were unable to guarantee that there would be accommodation for anyone who might eventually take her place. Other congregations who were asked were not in a position to send any of their members. Consequently, the school closed for good in July 1959.

A plan to rebuild the school did not materialise. When the establishment closed it had about a hundred children, of whom only seven were French pupils. These were then directed to the Lycée in Kensington. The others, especially the Italians and the Spanish, were accepted by the Catholic schools in the area, such as St. Patrick's in Soho, which welcomed ninety of them.

Father Yves Le Creurer was sent to London in 1949 to take care of the youth. He was welcomed by Rector with these blunt words: "*There is nothing for you* [to build on] *here; you will have to start from scratch.*"[193] Father Le Creurer was to go on and complete thirty years of pastoral service in Notre Dame de France

Father Le Creurer, then thirty years of age, enrolled in an English language course in the city. There he mixed with young French students, craftsmen, nannies, office workers or non-professionals who arrived in droves from the continent under the pretext of learning the language of the country. Despite the inhospitable Immigration Authorities and the strict control by Border Police, along with the immense difficulty in finding work, these young people did not seem to be dissuaded from travelling to London in search of a trade, a change of scenery or a new direction in life. Most of them did not know of the existence of a French parish. Helped by a young French volunteer Father Le Creurer started to make himself useful, doing his best to welcome, listen to and offer help. In 1950, with the aid of the Society of Charitable Works, he began a small social outreach programme which occupied two small rooms in the Holborn area, open to any young French whether they were Catholic or not. Thanks to the financial support of a group of businessmen the Charles Péguy Centre began in 1953 offering various services. For seven years it was based in a little house in Soho where there was room for a secretariat, a library, a bar, a meeting room and a club for dances or discussions. The final closure of the girls' school freed up almost 300 square metres in Leicester Square which the Charles Péguy Centre was then able to occupy and develop from 1960 onwards.

At the end of the 1950s, nearly 600 members took part in the various activities at the Charles Péguy Centre such as the cinema club, sight-seeing around London, concerts, and conferences organised by the Alliance Française or the French Institute. Some years later Christian Encounters were added to the list of activities. Prepared by Father Le Creurer these meetings involved Catholic personalities such as Henri de Lubac,[194] Maurice Zundel,[195] Jean Daniélou[196] and Jacques de Bollardière.[197] English intellectuals came in droves. Many others who were not active members in the Centre also took full advantage of these stimulating conferences.

The Charles Péguy Centre today

Today, the Centre has legal status in Great Britain as a non-profit association. It is subsidised by the French Ministry for Foreign Affairs and supported by the French Consulate in London. At the request of the Marist Fathers, the Centre of International Exchanges (CEI) took over the management of the Charles Péguy Centre in 1983. It remained at the premises in 16 Leicester Square until 2006 when it relocated to the vicinity of Waterloo Station. Since 2010 it has been located in Shoreditch.[198] In 2013 more than 10,000 visitors were received at the Centre and, using the services available there, around 1,000 young French people found jobs with French or British companies.

While the physical rebuilding of the church continued a closer collaboration of the Marists with the laity made possible the introduction of several charitable movements to Notre Dame de France. In 1951, under the guidance of Father André Huguet, the first team of *Independent Catholic Action* (ACI)[199] was formed. At the same time, inspired by the work of Father Henri Caffarel,[200] Father Huguet began groups[201] to nourish the spirituality of married couples. A number of families in the parish sought such pastoral direction and they founded the Teams of Our Lady which are still active in Notre Dame de France in 2015.

In 1951 *Our Lady of Walsingham Centre* was launched which offered workshops to assistant lecturers from French universities staying in London. They met each month for study days in a retreat house in London and finished the year with a pilgrimage to the Marian Shrine of Walsingham in Norfolk. The Marist Fathers took responsibility for the chaplaincy of the Centre. At the end of the 1950s around three hundred persons were actively involved in the Centre.

The *Conference of St Vincent de Paul*[202] had been in existence in Notre Dame de France since 1925. At the time it was run independently and under the responsibility of the parish. The Conference continued its work even through the difficult times. During the worst moments of the Blitz, Father Laurent wrote in his diary every Sunday evening: "*St. Vincent de Paul – to make my little offering*". Reasons for the Conference to continue its dedicated work were not lacking during the post-war years because large numbers of Londoners had lost everything.

A document addressed to the Consul General[203] drew up a review of the parish activities in 1959: "*Church Service: around 1,200 people each Sunday; 1959 – 76 baptisms, 45 marriages, 12 funerals. In the presbytery a Father is always on duty from 9 am until midday and from 2 pm until 7 pm. Hospital: Daily Mass and visits to the sick twice a week. French Lycée: two Fathers give religious instruction in perfect harmony with the school management from class 10 up to senior literature and language grade. Many English people attend the church for religious exercises. Quite a number of French speaking foreign nationals come to the church: Belgians, Italians...*"

This first decade after the war saw not only a strengthening of the links between the Marists and lay Christians, but also the beginning of their active participation and their responsibilities within the parish. This was an essential dimension of the Marist vision which continues to our day.

THE SECOND CHURCH: RECONSTRUCTION

IV. Recent Times

1. Growth and Changes 1960-1987

The 1960s would be a time of great change in the parish. In 1964 a trust was established to administer the funds and properties of Notre Dame de France necessary for its mission. According to the statutes of the trust these funds were to be managed by a board of Trustees who were appointed by the superior of the Marist community. The funds were to be used for the pastoral care of the French Catholics and the French speaking people of London. They would be under the control of the Charity Commission.

1.1. Mauritians and the African Communities

England has always welcomed people from the Commonwealth countries. Since the beginning of the 1950s increased immigration from many of these countries made London one of the most ethnically-diverse European cities.

In 1961 employment visas became obligatory and this appreciably slowed the flow of immigration. Still, 22,000 Mauritians emigrated to England between 1961 and 1982. Many were leaving their country for good and entire families settled in the country, the majority around London. Everything was new for those who arrived: the lifestyle, the rhythm of life, the climate, and the mentality. Sharing a French culture, it was natural for the Mauritians to turn to the French church in London.

From October 1964 four Mauritians[204] formed a small team with Father Daniel Raabe,[205] one of the Marists in Notre Dame de France as adviser. Jean Murat, now aged over 80 was one of the Mauritian pioneers. He recalls "...*Meeting regularly twice or three*

times a week we undertook to visit the London parishes... to help the increasing number of Mauritians to become part of the parishes where they lived. This work of integration lasted for two or three years..."[206]

Overall, this initial attempt to integrate the migrants into the local church was not a success. Integration did improve somewhat after Cardinal Heenan[207] wrote a pastoral letter recommending a more Christian welcome for all immigrants, regardless of their origin. In May 1968, eight Mauritians founded the Christian Association of Mauritians in London (ACML), "*more of a socio-cultural group with Constitutions, a President and a management committee*".[208]

In November of the same year the association numbered 195 members. This would increase to 470 ten years later, in 1978. The aim was to bring together the Mauritians based in London and provide a place for them to meet one another and pray in an atmosphere suitable to their traditions and customs. In short, to allow them maintain their identity. Their activities centred on the Sunday Mass with a Mauritian choir. They also had evening dances each month and excursions by bus in the summer. A monthly newsletter from Mauritius helped to spread news from home. The Marists of Notre Dame de France, through Father Groetz[209] who was chaplain and Honorary President of ACML, supported their activities and growth, thus ensuring the continued presence of Mauritians as French-speaking parishioners, and, later, as an association of the parish.

Mauritian immigration to Great Britain diminished from 1990 to 2000. Gradually the first generation of Mauritians became more and more rooted where they lived. Consequently many of their children chose to belong to Catholic parishes nearer their homes. Some, however, continued to come faithfully to the parish masses in Leicester Place. The ACML in London is still present in Notre Dame de France in 2015 with a membership of around 600.

Successive waves of migrants from francophone Africa, especially from Cameroon and Congo, came to London in the 1970s. More followed them from the Ivory Coast in the 1990s. Like the Mauritians before them, these African communities contributed to the growth of Notre Dame de France.

CHAPTER IV

Father Huguet emphasised "...*the legitimate place of churches devoted to the service of ethnic groups living in a foreign country. In fact, Notre Dame de France strives to respond in this way to provide spiritual service especially to the French but also to other francophone groups living in London. Our Sunday masses and the organisations which bring adults, young people or children together, try to re-create something of their experience... before coming to London*".[210]

1.2. The Centenary 1965

In 1965 it was the responsibility of the rector, Father Huguet, to organise the centenary of Notre Dame de France. A conference by René Varin[211] on the history of the parish opened the celebrations. An organ recital of French liturgical music,[212] a fundraising sale, an exposition of historical photos and a ticketed formal dinner celebration completed the programme.

The 25th March 1965 was both the anniversary of the church and the feast of the Annunciation. Two important religious ceremonies took place in the church on that day – the consecration of the new altar and a pontifical mass celebrated by the Archbishop of Westminster.[213] Cardinal Achille Lienart[214] gave the homily and the Apostolic Delegate to Great Britain[215] consecrated the new altar made of white Portland stone. In conformity with the recommendations of the recently ended Second Vatican Council it was placed in such a way that the celebrant was facing the congregation.

The anniversary was fittingly celebrated with the presence of many religious and civic leaders from both France and Great Britain reflecting Franco-British friendship. Above all, though, it was a gathering which reflected the ecumenical spirit inspired by the Second Vatican Council for many representatives of the different Christian communities in London were happy to participate in the Anniversary.

RECENT TIMES   65

1.3. New Directions for a Parish

This ecumenical spirit bore further fruit. In February 1970 the rector,[216] Father Noblet, hosted in Notre Dame de France historic discussions between Cardinal Marty, Archbishop of Paris and chairman of the French Episcopal Conference and Dr. Ramsey, Archbishop of Canterbury and Primate of the Anglican Communion. It was the first time since the Reformation that the French episcopacy paid an official visit to the Anglican community. This meeting followed on from the joint declaration signed in Rome in 1966 by Pope Paul VI and Dr. Ramsey. Cardinal Marty affirmed that he had not come to London to explore theological differences – that was the responsibility of a mixed commission established by the Secretariat for Christian Unity in Rome – but to have a *pastoral conversation*.

The two Archbishops presided over a liturgy together in Notre Dame de France which concluded with a double blessing given simultaneously, each in his own language. John Heenan, Archbishop of Westminster, assisted at the ceremony as did representatives of different Christian communities in London.[217]

The public in general had been given very little information about the presence of the French delegation. But the occasion allowed some Catholic voices to react, one Catholic Londoner remarked that, "*It is good to be able to point out to the Anglicans that the Catholic Church isn't only Italian and Irish.*"[218]

Father Gérard Noblet

Father Noblet began to implement the new guidelines from Rome, in particular those that recognised the laity as an integral part of the missionary Church. These guidelines benefitted Notre Dame de France greatly as it was a community of rich human diversity amongst young and less young lay people alike.

Some of this rich diversity was expressed in very individual ways! One regular parishioner in the 1960s and 1970s, would position herself in the pew she reckoned to be the most strategic before the beginning of mass. During the collection, which followed the sermon, she would raise her hand high waving a pound note if she was satisfied with what the priest had said or a penny if that were not the case.

There were also those who gave generously not counting their time, their energy or their support. The history of Notre Dame de France is the story of those tirelessly devoted women and men without whom the parish would not be what it is. Some have served the church for many decades. Michelle André was one such parishioner; she set up the Provencal Christmas crib for 50 years from 1947 to 1997.

Colette Moran of the St. Vincent de Paul Conference is another example. As government social services developed and hospitals increasingly took responsibility for treating a wider range of medical conditions, the need for assistance offered by the conference changed. In 1965 the Notre Dame de France Conference, which had no more than a dozen members at that time, devoted itself to bringing material support and encouragement to those in need – persons without means, the sick or the lonely. By the end of the 1990s the Conference could no longer remain independent and so was incorporated into the St. Vincent of Paul Society. In 1998 Colette Moran became the last president. She remembered that, "*In 1999-2000 we used to meet once a week in Notre Dame de France to decide (on what action to take)... We used to visit lonely French or Francophones in hospital, at home or in nursing homes. Each year we used to organise an outing by bus and a lunch for the retired and elderly – nearly 100 persons – in the parish hall of Notre Dame de France... Along with members belonging to other conferences I used to visit the prisons. In 2009 we were only three. For several years we were looking for new members but without success... After a final lunch we put an end to our conference.*"

RECENT TIMES   67

1.4. The Chaplaincy of the French Lycée

Father Noblet was asked to take care of the chaplaincy in 1965. He was known for his friendly way with young people. For fifteen years he had been chaplain to public and private establishments in France and had followed the evolution of the pastoral care of students. This ministry was no longer entrusted exclusively to priests or religious men and women but involved more and more lay persons.

The majority of chaplaincies in state schools carried out their various activities in locations outside of the schools. The chaplaincy of the Lycée worked in a different way. The enrolment of interested pupils passed through the administration of the Lycée. Catholic or Protestant instruction was given within school grounds by the Marists or the Pastor of the Reformed Church. Only authorised chaplains had such access to the Lycée. Classrooms could only be used within strictly limited hours and, even then, all posters of a religious nature were forbidden. It almost needed a miracle to arrange a parents meeting! Religious celebrations for the chaplaincy took place outside the Lycée in the cramped chapel of More House, a neighbouring Catholic chaplaincy.

At that time there were many small houses (*Mews*) next to the Lycée which were destined to be demolished sometime in the future. The French Institute bought them on the off-chance of expanding. The idea to install the chaplaincy there, at least temporarily, came from the parents of the pupils. An arrangement was reached with the management[220] whereby the small unoccupied building at 23 Cromwell Mews, which was without water or electricity, could be used provisionally by the chaplaincy for a very modest price. No contract was signed but it was understood that when the work of demolition resumed they would have to leave the place with one month's notice.

The interest of the parents and neighbours gradually developed. The scouts of Notre Dame de France cleaned and repainted the house, which was seriously dilapidated, but there was much more to be done before the first groups could begin to use it. At the start of the new school year in 1966 Father Jean Noël Bozon was sent from France as extra support. With Father Noblet he followed the ups and downs of the chaplaincy at 23 Cromwell Mews for fifteen years until, one day, a proper lease was arranged with the solicitor – a lease which is still valid today.

Having found a home the first step was to start teaching catechism 'in the French way' and to recruit catechists. *"The parents did not expect to be asked to do a job which they had never envisaged. I remember my first interview with a mother who very soon turned out to be a remarkable catechist. Madame B. said to me: "You are dreaming, Father! It is you who ought to teach me".*[221] After a relatively short delay some 500 pupils from 1st form to the upper 6th were being instructed by more than fifty lay catechists both men and women.

68   CHAPTER IV

Catechism was not limited to religious instruction. The young people were evangelised and initiated into the fraternal life of a small community which they were able to develop through the chaplaincy. A weekly mass was arranged for the second cycle (high-school) students. Given the limited size of the place it was necessary occasionally to rely on the hospitality of a neighbouring community – the priest of St. Augustine's Anglican parish near the Lycée opened the doors of his church to the students.

"*One of the things most necessary for the spiritual and civic formation of the students is to invite them to make retreats in quality surroundings.*"[222] For one-day retreats the youth of the chaplaincy went to the Marist Sisters, on Fulham Road, or to the Daughters of Charity near Westminster Cathedral. For retreats lasting several days they stayed with the White Fathers in Dorking or in Totteridge in the north of London or with the religious of London Colney near St. Albans.

While Fathers Noblet and Bozon developed considerably the chaplaincy at Cromwell Mews they never neglected Notre Dame de France. They always celebrated Sunday Mass, the important liturgies of the year and the National Feast-days, the first Communions, Professions of Faith and the Confirmations at Notre Dame de France. For many of the older students of the chaplaincy Notre Dame de France was their church where they assembled to participate in leading the liturgy or to direct the choir for the Sunday congregation.

As for the scout movement there was much to be done. 23 Cromwell Mews became a place for them to meet while helping with the renovations. Father Noblet wanted to revive the scout movement and in 1965 proposed to the parents to found a new unit. The national president of the Scouts of France[223] who was in London at that time welcomed the newly formed group into the movement.

New team leaders were yet to be formed: "*In the seminary of the White Fathers in Totteridge there are French students who are preparing to go on English-speaking Missions. Their superior agrees to put at our disposal former scout leaders. The chaplaincy is showing new growth and a new lease of life. The scout troop keeps in contact with Notre Dame de France through the chaplaincy*".[224]

The International Scout Museum of Baden Powell House[225] nearby was happy to welcome the Scouts of France and it was easy to arrange a meeting with the parents of the chaplaincy students. In 1968 the Scout movement for boys was well developed but nothing yet existed for girls. Fathers Noblet and Bozon proposed a movement for Girl Guides to Jacqueline Monnier, a parishioner of Notre Dame de France and directress of the International Bureau of Girl Guides in London. She advised the two Marists to go to the Headquarters of the Girl Guides of France. There it was suggested that the Fathers adapt a recent initiative in which a branch for girls over fifteen was created under the name of *Caravelles*. The idea of *Caravelles* was welcomed with enthusiasm by the students from Year 10 to the Final Year and it began to flourish at the chaplaincy. Sometime later Father Bozon launched the branch of junior girl guides and they had their first outing in the countryside. It was also a complete success.

For years the chaplaincy of the French Lycée collaborated with the chaplaincy of Pastor Dubois from the Protestant church in Soho. They organised many joint-meetings with students from both Lycées, in particular during Lent. Some of Pastor Dubois' parishioners would participate regularly in meetings in Notre Dame de France with a certain number attending Mass.

Gerard Noblet's teaching skills but, even more, his vision of pastoral care made him a key figure in the parish. At his request Father Wernert came from France on many occasions to give retreats for Confirmation and Profession of Faith before succeeding him as Rector[226] in 1981: *"I saw him working so hard trying to figure out how best to serve the young people in the chaplaincy and to help the community implement the ecumenical and liturgical changes of the Second Vatican Council which had just finished. After his departure, when we were discussing with Fathers Courson, Bozon and Groetz, possible or necessary changes to our pastoral work, we always arrived at the same conclusion that what Father Gerard had initiated was the right way and we would have to follow it..."*[227]

The chaplaincy at 23 Cromwell Mews was Father Noblet's legacy. There were fifty lay catechists, annual retreats for every level of Catechism,[228] prayers and hymns for Sunday Masses in Notre Dame de France – led by a roster of young students from different levels and directed by their Catechists – plus the troop of Scouts and the Guides who were so committed and full of life.

70   CHAPTER IV

1.5 A New Wave of French in London

From the 1980s onwards London increasingly became the financial centre of Europe. As such it became the ideal base for European insurance companies, the oil industry and major law firms. Inevitably, French commercial and legal institutions began to also establish themselves there. Middle and top executives of the French commercial and financial institutions were often sent to London for periods of at least three to five years.

These executives, mainly from the middle classes and often Catholics, settled in London with their families, generally in Kensington or in the adjacent neighbourhoods. They met for mass on Sunday in Notre Dame de France which helped them maintain links with their culture and values. These families, known as expats, from very similar backgrounds, knew each other like one big family. Their children were enrolled in the Lycée where the numbers were increasing. The school roll increased from 1,800 in 1958 to 2,200 in 1973 and then to 2,500 in 1980. The chaplaincy grew in proportion. As demand for French schooling in London continued to grow, the Jacques Prévert School, opened in 1974 in Brook Green[229] for primary school pupils.

In the 1970s and 1980s the Mauritian Association was very strong and the Charles Péguy Centre continued to organise social and cultural activities for the young French. At the same time the St. Vincent de Paul Conference, the Our Lady of Walsingham Centre and the A.C.I. were not as active as they had been. The French Hospital,[230] in which the Marist Fathers had always worked as chaplains, had to close down fifteen years[231] earlier than anticipated because of financial difficulties. It had served exactly one hundred years.[232]

Several Marists would soon leave Notre Dame de France having worked there for many years. Among them was Father Yves Le Creurer who left in 1979 after thirty years of service. He was followed two years later by Father Noblet. In July 1981 the Marist community consisted of the rector, Father Wernert, Fathers Bozon and Courson who were responsible for the chaplaincy at the Lycée and Father Groetz who was mainly responsible for the Mauritian community.

During the years 1981-1987, the Marists continued to reflect upon the pastoral work they were offering in the very heart of London. Aware that they were also ministering to English speakers – the midday Mass in English attracted significant numbers of people working in the area and confessions during the week remained important – they considered a chaplaincy for the people involved in the worlds of entertainment and journalism.[233] However, the project never took off.

In 1984 Father Groetz left London after sixteen years of ministry there. In 1986 the Provincial of France decided to withdraw the Marist Fathers from Notre Dame de France. Father Joel Bozon returned that year to France and Fathers Courson and Wernert followed him at the end of the summer of 1987.

RECENT TIMES

2. Notre Dame de France without the Marists 1987-1992

In the absence of replacements from the Society of Mary, the Directorate General of French Foreign Chaplaincies (DGAFE)[234] delegated Raymond Jovenez,[235] a Diocesan priest from the Diocese of Paris, to take over the parish of Leicester Place. The Marists retained a presence through the members of the Trust, and through its secretary, Yolande Cantu.

Some differences of approach between Father Jovenez and the parish community led to a diminishment in attendance at church and in involvement in the school chaplaincy. Fr Jovenez began a ministry to the prisons with some young volunteers, and he also devoted much energy to the Soho Centre Point project, launching inter-aid action with other churches of the area to help the homeless. He maintained a small choir to sing at the Sunday Mass and, seeing the church deserted, encouraged African communities to come in greater numbers. When his mandate was not renewed Father Jovenez returned to France.

Yolande Cantu & Father Jacques Coupet o.p.

The Trust secretary, Yalonde Cantu[236] – an expert translator and writer for the British Council and a faithful parishioner – tried by every means possible, including diplomatic circles, to convince the religious authorities at the highest level, to bring about the return of the Marists to Notre Dame de France. Without the determination and the firm insistence of Yolande Cantu and Bernadette Rattigan, another devoted parishioner, "*there would have been a complete rupture between the departure and the return of the Marists to Notre Dame de France. Thanks to them and some others, a certain continuity was maintained.*"[237] With the support of the Embassy[238] and the Superior General of the Marists, the DGAFE persuaded the Dominican Jacques Coupet to take over the mission of Leicester Place while the Society of Mary was forming a new team.

At that time, Father Coupet had been living in London for years as his superiors had suggested that he present a doctoral thesis[239] to the Sorbonne on Cardinal John Henry Newman's correspondence. A long friendship linked him to the French Marists, who, on more than one occasion, invited him to preach at the Sunday Mass. He had for so long a time been part of the life of the church that the parishioners almost saw him as a member of the Marist community. He did however maintain his independence.[240]

After the departure of the Marists in 1987, Father Coupet was there to ensure the continuance of a spirit which he appreciated. On the departure of Father Jovenez Father Coupet was installed as rector, a position he would keep until the return of the Marists in 1992. He was helped in his task by a number of devoted parishioners among whom were Paule Bechno and Collette Moran. During this period, Maria Refig played a key role in continuing the chaplaincy work.[241] She taught catechism and soon became the soul of the chaplaincy upon which the little parish team concentrated. To organise the retreats Jacquet Coupet asked Father Noblet to return, as his particular talent in speaking to the young students about the Gospel gradually brought them back to 23 Cromwell Mews.

3. The Return of the Marists 1992-2015

3.1. New Perspectives, New Engagements

The Superior General of the Marists asked the Provincial Superiors of France, England and Ireland to supply men to form the new team. In 1992 a new international community of Marist Fathers arrived in London: Clive Birch from England who became rector and religious superior, Walter Gaudreau from America and Paul Walsh from Ireland. The Marists gave a lot of thought to the circumstances and conditions of the parish upon their return. What meaning might a Marist Mission in London have at a time when so much had changed? How could one evaluate as accurately as possible the changes and identify the immediate needs? What manpower resources had the Society to face up to the mission? How best explore the ways to evangelise?

The Marist community and the entire parish responded to these new challenges by focusing their mission and actions on a welcoming ministry, the poor, formation and evangelisation. Putting structures in place for the welcoming ministry became necessary and the active participation of the laity increased.

A **Welcoming Room** was organised to receive visitors who needed a listening ear or who were looking for spiritual direction. A place was reserved for this in the interior of the church and a team of trained volunteers was available each day. The doors of Notre Dame de France remained open until late into the night, particularly for such occasions as *Night Church* – an evening of welcoming and prayer.

Ecumenical initiatives were developed with the French Protestant church in Soho Square and the other Christian parishes in the neighbourhood. Taizé, an international prayer group, which used English, was founded in 1993 at the initiative of representatives from neighbouring parishes who wished to bring young people together. Father Paul Walsh, youth chaplain for the deanery, with a team coming from the nearby parishes started to gather the young people in Notre Dame de France for periods of prayer and informal exchanges. The Taizé initiative gradually evolved attracting people from different denominations and parishes.

The parish began to experience a period of renewal. This required an adaptation of its structures and a co-ordination of many of its activities. On the initiative of Clive Birch the **Parish Council** was formed representing various groups and activities. Its mission was to explore the needs and available resources for evangelisation. On the other hand the **Pastoral Team**, which was composed of Marist priests and lay people, guaranteed the balance in decisions taken concerning the mission and the community. The Parish Assembly held twice a year brought together religious and those lay-people who directed activities in the parish. The aim was to promote communion between the numerous elements which were part of this vast parish scattered over the whole of London. This dimension of communion was also emphasised by the annual **Parish Feast** which had been reintroduced.

Father Bernard Boisseau, who succeeded John Collier as rector, launched a new project: *Notre Dame Village*. The term meant an extended community uniting the Marists and a group of young lay people living on the premises in the Tower[242] near the presbytery. They joined with the Fathers in prayer, shared time with them and helped with certain apostolic responsibilities in the parish.

Engaging lay-people in running the parish, coupled with the generosity of many parents involved with the Lycée and other volunteers, helped to mould a vibrant, diverse and innovative community.

Changes were also made to the building in order to better serve the constantly evolving mission. In 1998, Notre Dame de France had been classified by English Heritage as a grade II building shortly before substantial restoration work and interior decoration was to be carried out. It was then that the liturgical space in the church was reorganised to bring it into conformity with the post-conciliar reforms. The architect, Gerard Murphy, erected an oval shaped platform in the middle of the sanctuary as a base for the original altar which previously had been positioned on top of several high steps. The two lecterns were removed and placed to the side while the communion rail was transferred to the chapel of the Blessed Virgin. A new lectern was installed on the platform and a niche was built behind the sanctuary for the tabernacle.

The organ, a unique instrument in England because of its French tone, was modified and improved upon by Shepherd and Son in 2010.[243] The present organist, Duncan Middleton, adds

RECENT TIMES

to the instrument's international reputation. Ways of communication were improved by rebuilding the website, remodelling the logo, and establishing new branding. Two brochures about the tapestry of Dom Robert and the murals of Jean Cocteau were printed in 2007. Weekly bulletins and a quarterly magazine are made available to visitors at the entrance to the church where notice boards are regularly updated.

3.2 New Initiatives and Communities

To meet the needs of the numerous young French students or professionals who continued to arrive in London throughout the 1980s the parish formed groups for reflection and prayer, working with the scouts and a choir. One such group is the **Gaudete** group which began in 2009. The members animate a mass each month and provide sessions for training and reflection.

Activities for all ages and every circumstance were begun: marriage preparation teams, prayer groups (e.g. charismatic, Ignatian prayer, groups simply for reflection and sharing), music and liturgical teams and the **Ecumenical Bible Study Group** with the Protestant church.[244] The catechumenate for adults and the **Sunday School** were also developed further.

At the request of a group of parents from the chaplaincy Saturday masses in French were introduced in Christ Church[245] in Kensington. This Anglican church made an agreement with Notre Dame de France for the use of the church – still in force in 2015 – for the benefit of the French settled in the west of London. Monthly or quarterly masses are celebrated in the more distant areas of Clapham, Ealing or Fulham.

The parish introduced the Alpha course in French. This course was later to be introduced in France by the Emmanuel community with the help of Marc and Florence de Leiritz, parishioners of Notre Dame de France who had returned to France.

The **African communities** went through important changes and increased significantly. Quite a number of the Africans present in Notre Dame de France in the 1990s were Congolese. At that time one mass each month was being celebrated in the Zairian rite (using Lingala, the language of the country) which included processions, liturgical dances and chants. From 2008 the Congolese had their own chaplain who celebrated this rite each Sunday in a parish in the north of London. Because of this fewer came to Notre Dame de France but the parish still maintained a very friendly relationship with their chaplain. When the Marists returned in 1992, the Ivorian, Venance Djouka, was directing an African choir with members from the Cameroons, Congo and the Ivory Coast. They sang at the 11.30 a.m. mass on Sundays. Jonas Tiero, also from the Ivory Coast, eventually succeeded Venance Djouka. In 2008 Salomon Bakoa from Cameroon took over responsibility for the choir. He is still in charge in 2015.

In 1997, with the help of Mathurin Zeze and other African parishioners, Father Michel Desvignes[246] formed a prayer group which undertook to read together the Gospel of St. John. The group was called **Word and Life** (Parole et Vie) and is still active in 2015. They started an annual two-day pilgrimage of 150 persons to the Marian shrine of Walsingham,[247] a Christmas Tree Celebration for children and a football tournament for the older ones. Other groups appeared later on – in particular **Notre Dame de Refuge**, a charismatic prayer group expressing itself in the less formal, more expressive style of worship and evangelising activity appreciated by the Africans. The group meets every Sunday afternoon in the church as it became too big for the parish centre. Several other prayer groups have been created in London by members of Notre Dame de Refuge.

Magnificat came from a group launched in the 1990s by students and young professionals who were members of the Emmanuel community, and then reorganised by Father Desvignes as a school of prayer. It was not originally an initiative of the African communities, even though today the majority of those taking part are African.

Another charismatic group, **Ephphata**, born in Cameroon and also present in France, has been meeting since 2003 for prayer and adoration on Thursday evenings. Aware of the need for the evangelisation and catechesis of the young, somewhat neglected after their First Communion, some young members of Notre Dame de Refuge founded **The Apostles**.

This group, composed of young adults from several continents, spends time in prayer and faith sharing on Wednesday evenings in the church. All these groups meet at mass on Sundays, in particular at the 11.30 a.m. celebration which brings together a multi-cultural community of French, Africans, Mauritians and people from other nations.

On the 15th April 2012, the French TV program *The Day of the Lord* broadcast the mass live on France 2 channel placing Notre Dame de France in the limelight and enabling it to reach a wider audience.

3.3 Service to the Homeless

While Notre Dame de France is a parish overflowing with activities and initiatives it remains no less open to the outside world and its mission to the more deprived.

In 1993 sandwiches were already being distributed to the homeless at the door of the presbytery to those who found themselves in the streets because of unemployment, or some personal, familial or social crises. As the demand for this service grew volunteers from the parish helped by four Marist Sisters,[248] took over responsibility from the priests.

Today there is a **Sandwich Service** each Saturday in the parish centre from 12.30 to 2.30 p.m. Volunteers welcome up to 180 guests who receive something to eat and drink but, even more importantly, have the opportunity to chat and rest for a few hours.

Every year during the winter months[249] Notre Dame de France is a partner in the **Cold Weather Night Shelter** programme.[250] One evening each week a team of volunteers receives fifteen or so homeless people in the parish centre and gives them dinner, a warm, safe place to sleep and breakfast next morning. In turn, other parishes of different denominations in the Westminster borough undertake to provide the same sort of accommodation for the remaining nights of the week.

3.4. The Notre Dame Refugee Centre

With the widening of its horizons, it is not only the French or Francophone communities which are served by the parish. There is now an international dimension to the outreach activities of the parish, in particular through the creation of the Refugee Centre.

In 1995, in line with its mission to welcome everyone and more particularly to defend the poorest and the excluded, Notre Dame de France joined with other religious communities and community organisations to protest vigorously against the tightening of the immigration law and the limiting of requests for political asylum in England. The parish participated in the formation of an interreligious network in the centre of London which focused on defending the rights of refugees and, together with other Christian communities in the area, it became involved in lobbying members of parliament. It also became an part of a consultative group of the Catholic Bishops of England and Wales for the protection of immigrants and refugees.

The Notre Dame Refugee Centre was created in 1996 with the help of some refugees and a team of volunteers from the parish. Father Paul Walsh was the first director and held that position until he left in 1999. Paid lay directors succeeded him[251] thus guaranteeing the future of the Centre while preserving its fundamental values – offering a friendly familial welcome to refugees. In the year 2000 the running of the Centre was almost entirely in the hands of volunteers, mothers from the Lycée and some other volunteers, the majority of whom had connections with Notre Dame de France. In 2015, this is no longer the case since the Centre has grown considerably. It has been entrusted, for the most part, to professionals from outside the parish, some of whom receive salaries, as well as to volunteers from different places.

In the 1990s most of the refugees and asylum seekers who came to the centre were French speaking. Today they come from every country, of diverse ages and beliefs. Each week the centre receives more than 100 visitors who stand in need of just about everything to live their lives – food, clothing, English language classes and courses in other skills essential in adapting to the unknowns of life in England. The refugees can also meet with interpreters and professional counsellors who help them in the administrative steps required in finding accommodation and employment.

The contribution of volunteers, both men and women, from the parish and elsewhere, all offering their own skills and experience, has formed a link, a connection between the refugees and the expatriate French community, apparently so far apart from each other. One tangible expression of this link is the fundraising and the food collection done by the children and young people from the school chaplaincy.

At the end of the 1990s however, the charitable projects undertaken by the Marists to help the refugees and other individuals in distress were deemed not to be in conformity with the 1964 Deed creating the Trust of Notre Dame de France. This stipulated that the mission of Notre Dame de France was specifically for the French community. To be able to continue these initiatives the wording of the Deed had to be changed. So, from being a French parish Notre Dame de France now legally became a *Francophone* parish. With this modification the Trust was able to continue its role of support and guarantor of the activities of the parish as they had developed over time.

In 2006, the Charles Péguy Centre managed by the CEI[253] left 16 Leicester Square for good. The former location of the parish school was renamed the Peter Chanel[254] Centre. It would act as the parish centre accommodating prayer groups, the Saturday sandwich service, the night shelter for the homeless and other activities. Since 1999 the Refugee Centre had occupied part of the building but in 2006 it moved its offices to the third floor. The Refugee Centre is now managed by an independent Trust. This arrangement allows it to be independent and helps to facilitate the appeal for funds. The centre maintains strong links with the parish through the Board of Trustees who are together with others, also trustees of the Centre.

3.5. The School Chaplaincy

In 2015 the French community in London numbers around 300,000. The children are educated in various schools spread across the city. Notre Dame de France provides religious instruction for eight French schools. Graded into four levels almost 1,000 children from the age of 6 to 18 are enrolled in the chaplaincy. Members of the Marist team are the chaplains. There is a paid coordinator and around one hundred volunteer catechists.

The numbers of high-school students make it impossible to go on retreats all together. Common retreats are replaced by smaller groups going away for two or three weekends in the year. Once a month there is a time for sharing at the homes of couples who are trained for this purpose. These couples take up to ten children at a time for a meal and then share some thoughts on a theme or a subject of interest regarding the faith of the young people. Since 2005/2006, students from the Lycée have been taking part in the Frat, an annual youth festival attended by the chaplaincies of schools in the Greater Paris region.

The chaplaincy prepares children for the sacraments which they receive in Notre Dame de France. In terms of the number of pupils enrolled and the number of catechists it is the biggest chaplaincy for any French school in France or in the world.

Although attached to the chaplaincy and the parish the scout movement remains independent. Accompanied spiritually by a chaplain from Notre Dame de France it has its own administrative structure and its own separate management structure.

3.6. Presence and Evangelisation in the West End

Because of its exceptional location in the heart of London Notre Dame de France is ideally placed to respond to the call of the Church to bear witness to Christ and to evangelise. It is in the entertainment district of the West End and so is jammed with tourists and full of life throughout the year. In response to an invitation from the Westminster Diocese the four

Catholic parishes[255] of the West End launched several initiatives of direct evangelisation in 2006 coordinated by Anne Marie Salgo.

Spirit in the City is one of the key evangelisation programmes. It is an annual festival which is supported by the Archbishop of Westminster[256] and takes place in summer for four days in the churches of the West End and the public spaces in the area. Through prayer and music, combined with talks, processions, workshops and theatre, it celebrates the rich Catholic life and faith of the different parish communities, individuals and ecclesial movements which take part in it. Sharing the joy of the Gospel with the contemporary world is at the heart of this event. It finds its vitality in the participation of more than 200 volunteers from all over London and elsewhere.

The Catholic churches of Soho and the West End have set up a **Listening Service** made available for the gay community, their families and friends. A dedicated telephone line ensures anonymity and confidentiality to those who call and offers them the opportunity to meet with a priest.

Other initiatives emerged, such as the annual *Advent Mission* with St. Patrick's in Soho or the monthly street outreach of *LumiNations*. **Night Church** twice a month offers an oasis of peace, prayer and beauty to passers-by who may wish to enter the church and light a candle.

In this way, the Notre Dame de France team seeks to find ways and means to share Christian values in an environment devoted to entertainment and theatre. Several such artistic events with Christian themes have been staged on its premises, e.g. a play written by St. John Paul II,[257] another[258] based on the life of St. Maximillian Kolbe (both were performed by the Catholic drama company "Ten Ten Theatre"), and a more recent play based on the life of John Newton who composed the hymn, *Amazing Grace*.[259] The church has also hosted art exhibitions, such as the religious paintings of Elizabeth Wang and the paintings and sculptures of the visitors from the Refugee Centre.

3.7. A Parish with a Difference

Notre Dame de France occupies a unique position because of its geographical, human and spiritual situation. It is situated at the crossroads of the nations, where individuals and families from all parts of the city, and of the planet meet together, as indicated by the number of national flags hanging from the façade of the church.[260]

The major challenge for the mission is to join up the diverse elements of which it is composed. It means, in effect, opening up the different parts of this community to one another in order to establish a bridge between them or better still, to create a sense of communion and of mission. Over and beyond getting material assistance, the challenge remains to arouse a truly personal commitment.

By its size, its complexity, by the nature and diversity of its mission, through the exceptional and renewed commitment of the laity, and finally by the totality of fundamental values of the Marist commitment, Notre Dame de France is, indeed, a unique parish.

RECENT TIMES

Afterword

Notre Dame de France is celebrating its 150th birthday. It has lived through a period of history that could hardly be richer and more diverse: the period of great empires of the modern world and their demise; two world wars, with many less global conflicts, but with immense consequences for the French-speaking world; the birth and decline of nationalism; the arrival of mighty totalitarian projects and their collapse; economic globalisation and the closing of frontiers; affluence and starvation; nuclear and environmental threats and advanced awareness of planetary solidarity; explosion of technology and helplessness in the face of political and social crises; the greatest experiment in multinational democracy in Europe and the unparalleled migration of people throughout the world; the death of religion as we have known it and the rise of fundamentalism and extremism in religious beliefs … Thanks to its privileged location in the very heart of London, urban capital of the modern world, Notre Dame de France has always found itself facing these challenges for human society. In rereading its history we have the opportunity to feel in miniature something of the echoes and impact of these 150 years of humanity.

From its inception, Notre Dame de France has been caught up in the human, social and spiritual consequences of such global events in accompanying displaced and vulnerable populations throughout the 150 years of its existence. This history allows us to grasp and give thanks for this rich adventure. The story begins with the invitation offered by the Archbishop of Westminster in 1860 to the small community of Marist Fathers in the east of London, asking them to look after the pastoral needs of the poor French of Soho. These pages present us with several examples of the pitiable state of the French living in the area. It leads us up to 2015, where the Marists, and their myriad partners in mission, continue to respond to the pastoral needs of the present day: the French and French-speaking Africans and their families arriving in London in search of new opportunities and a new life; the critical situation facing refugees and the homeless, all those seeking a meaning for their life and a place for them in the society of today. In these pages we can see the points of continuity. We can also see what is new in the circumstances of our time.

In the course of these pages you will discover the vision and effort of men and women who conceived, built and developed Notre Dame de France throughout its history, a history marked by the courage and generosity of individuals, by the cooperation and team-work of different groups: the people and governments of Britain and France, along with French and French-speaking immigrants; Marist Fathers, Sisters, and Brothers and other religious communities; the dioceses of Westminster and of France, and a constantly renewed pool of talented and generous volunteers who form a partnership with the religious and together constitute a wonderful missionary team. Thanks to the contribution of these people and of these entities, we are today able to enjoy a community that is rich in its diversity, a series of programmes enriching in undeniable ways the lives of thousands of people, and buildings made beautiful with works of art and filled with spirituality.

The Marists and the many teams today serving the mission of Notre Dame de France propose to continue and to develop this fine tradition. The Christian education of children and of youth; the formation and support of adult Christians; the spreading of the joy of the Gospel in London's West End and in other parts of this huge city; a place of refuge and of encounter for the poor and the exiled; a warm welcome for all passers by; an ally for each person and every community seeking to make the city a more human space. The Marist Fathers in Europe are committed to developing this work of mission, recognising it as one of their pastoral priorities in the coming years. Notre Dame de France is a key player in the world-wide Marist network of city-centre missions – in response to the recent Popes inviting Christian communities to engage in the "new Aeropagi" where the joy of the gospel can best be shared with the people of our time and of the emerging future. There is every hope that those coming to Notre Dame de France in the coming decades will enthusiastically engage with this wonderful mission, ensuring that its future will prove just as rich and fruitful as its past. It is our hope that, reading these pages, you will find emerge within your heart a desire to be associated with the work of Notre Dame de France.

Paul Walsh,
s.m. Rector

Notes

1. Five of whom were daughters of Kings of France.
2. The Parliamentary debates are translated into English for the first time in 1362.
3. In Français et Britanniques (French and British) by Jean Etevenaux, Edition Fabrica Libri 2010, p.109.
4. The year in which William III of Orange Nassau overthrew his father-in-law, the Catholic King James II.
5. The Royal Bounty which will be distributed to them until 1804.
6. Two centuries later this business-like attitude would play a major role in the development of capitalism.
7. The first French Protestant Church was built in London in 1550.
8. In London but also around Canterbury, Southampton and Norwich.
9. In 1661 Charles II offers the Huguenots the little Savoy chapel and the Greek Church in London. In 1681 he grants them legal status authorising them to freely practise their professions and business.
10. The United Provinces, England, Geneva, and the Swiss cantons, the German Catholic principalities.
11. The Huguenot weavers hold exclusive rights to manufacture Cardinals' hats in the Vatican!
12. The corporations.
13. A fine stone house with an attic, nine windows on the façade and a garden in front, with enough space in the back to hold military manoeuvres.
14. Charles I.
15. Brother of the Great Colbert (1619-1683) Louis XIV's minister.
16. Princess Elizabeth, who became Queen of Bohemia and died in Leicester House in 1662.
17. Frederick of Hanover, Prince of Wales (1707-1751).
18. Perhaps in the Lettres Anglaises, 1734, quotation not found.
19. In 1775 Leicester House was occupied by naturalist Ashton Lever's collection, mainly curiosities brought back by navigator and explorer Captain Cook (1728-1779).
20. W. Hogarth, J. Reynolds and T.H. Lawrence. What was Hogarth House became the Sablonnière Hotel a little later. The proprietor, M. Pagliano, was one of the donors when Notre Dame was founded. The Sablonnière Hotel was destroyed in 1870.
21. James Wyld (1817-1887).
22. The globe measured 19 m in diameter.
23. It was built in Moorish style and measured 32 m in height.
24. Robert Baker (1739-1806).
25. Etymologically a view which takes in everything.
26. For a shilling.
27. Distemper painting coming from sketches made following the design.

28. 10th January 1792.

29. Les Français à Londres de Guillaume Le Conquérant au Général de Gaulle [The French in London from William the Conqueror to General de Gaulle], by Isabelle Janvrin and Catherine Rawlinson, Bibliomane Editions. Paris 2013.

30. The Civil Constitution of Clergy was voted on 23rd July 1790, reorganising the secular clergy, but was not recognised by Pope Pius VI.

31. About thirty Bishops.

32. The alms shilling granted by the English government to the impoverished French priests until 1801, at which time the latter started to return to France.

33. The conflict lasted from 1793 to 1815, except for the brief period of the Amiens peace in 1802.

34. The control would be applied until 1801, when the refugees started returning to France.

35. Around St. George's Fields, today in Southwark.

36. The agreement was signed on 15th July 1801 in Paris between the First Consul Napoleon Bonaparte and the Papal Envoy of Pope Pius VI. The official recognition of Protestantism in 1802, then Judaism in 1808 put an end to religious fighting in France.

37. Signed on the 25th March 1802. In the spring of the following year England went to war again against Napoleon's France, lasting until 1815.

38. Until around 1815.

39. Compiled by Alfred Hamonet, W. Jeffs Editor, London 1862.

40. Such as Louis Blanc or Ledru-Rollin in 1851.

41. From one million around 1800 it would reach 6.7 million at the end of the century. This change was due to rural emigration to which one must add an influx of Irish immigrants during the famine years of 1840 due to the potato blight. The Irish immigrants gathered in the slums of the East End, near the docks.

42. The SFB, still very active today; it is the oldest of the French associations in Great Britain.

43. The CSVP is a lay association with the spirituality of serving the poor, directed by volunteers and founded in 1833 in Paris by Frédéric Ozanam. Their first President in London was M. Pagliano, proprietor of the Sablonnière Hotel, situated opposite Notre Dame de France church of which he was a generous protector.

44. William Thackeray in The Adventures of Philip on his way through the World, chapter 21, 1862, quoted by Isabelle Janvrin and Catherine Rawlinson in Les Français à Londres de Guillaume Le Conquérant au Général de Gaulle [The French in London from William the Conqueror to General de Gaulle], p.139.

45. Reference not found for the passage, quoted in Notre Dame de France 1965 centenary booklet.

46. Isabelle Janvrin and Catherine Rawlinson, 2013, p.139.

47. From that date the poor and sick French received free medical care immediately.

48. Isabelle Janvrin and Catherine Rawlinson, 2013, p.7.

49. Canon Toursel.

50. Cardinal Wiseman (1802-1865).

51. Cardinal Wiseman was appointed in 1850. Before then, Vicars Apostolic used to replace the hierarchy as in mission countries.

52. The blight, a mushroom from Mexico, which ravaged the potato harvest in Ireland for 10 years from 1845.

53. Founded in 1816 by a group of Marist Fathers among whom were Jean Claude Colin and Marcellin Champagnat.
54. At the same time, according to the region, lay ideas were more radical.
55. Pauline Jaricot (1799-1862).
56. Outside of France, the first move for the Marists Fathers was to England then Ireland, before spreading to the majority of Western European countries, to Norway and Italy.
57. It is said that Cardinal Wiseman travelled incognito to Paris and, without an appointment, met with the Superior of the Society of Mary to get his help to create a second mission in London for the benefit of the French of Leicester Square.
58. Cardinal Wiseman's appeal to the French bishops, 1861.
59. Charles Faure was born in Bordeaux in 1825. Ordained a priest in 1845, he was received into the Society of Mary in 1850.
60. In 1629 Louis XIII paid for the construction of the church in the convent of the Augustinian Brothers. They were expelled during the Revolution and the Church was turned into a cattle market.
61. Abbot Dufriche Desgenettes.
62. Cardinal Wiseman to Charles Faure 1861 date incomplete.
63. Cardinal Wiseman's appeal to the Bishops 1861.
64. Founded on the 3rd May 1822 in Lyon, the Propagation of the Faith Charity wished to support the Catholic Missions which had urgent needs, for the crisis at the end of the 18th century and the Revolutionary period had left them abandoned. They collected funds, prayed for the Christians on the Mission and gathered enthusiasm for the evangelisation through the publication of Nouvelles des Missions [Mission News].
65. Cardinal Wiseman to the Presidents of the Offices of the Propagation of the Faith in Paris and Lyons, Lyon 24th May 1862.
66. 28 m in diameter and 17.5 m in height.
67. The last two huge paintings of the Panorama, one representing Rome, the other Naples.
68. A note sent by Cardinal Wiseman to the President of the Propagation of the Faith in Lyons 6th May 1864.
69. From the letter of Francis(?- illegible signature) to Father Faure, London 5th May 1864: it concerns the English intermediary assisting Father Faure in the negotiations for the purchase of the Panorama.
70. Cardinal Wiseman to the President of Propagation of the Faith , London 28th June 1864.
71. Cardinal Wiseman.
72. Notes from Charles Faure to the Superior of the Marists 1865 date incomplete.
73. Robert Burford (1792-1861) painter of the Panoramas, succeeded Robert Barker's son and was director of the Royal Panorama of Leicester Square from 1827 until his death. The attraction was no longer in use after it was bought by Father Faure for Notre Dame de France.
74. Extract from a printed leaflet distributed to the participants of the Malines Congress: a major reunion of thinkers, laity and some eminent members of the Catholic Clergy, 1863.
75. Notre Dame de France archive.
76. Cardinal Manning's letter to Father Faure, London 11th August 1865.
77. Louis-Auguste Boileau (1821- 1896).
78. Churches of St. Eugene and St Cecilia in Paris (1854-1856) and St. Marguerite in Vésinet (1862-1865).

79. Notre Dame de France is the first church constructed of iron in London.
80. Charles Barry (1795-1860). The reconstruction of the Parliament would take place at intervals between the years 1840 to 1870.
81. Auguste Pugin (1812-1852) son of a French immigrant.
82. 62 King William Street, City of London.
83. On the ground floor in 16 Leicester Square, a former lecture room used by members of the Ultra Radical and Red Republican parties.
84. Extract from an unsigned article published in the Catholic magazine The Weekly Register, December 1865
85. Consecrated to the Blessed Sacrament, to Our Lady of Victories and to St. Joseph.
86. Printed: Notre Dame de France in London, appeal for funds, London 20th April 1868.
87. The church was dedicated to the Virgin Mary under the name of Notre Dame des Victoires. Therefore the titular is Notre Dame des Victoires whereas the title of the work or the mission is Notre Dame de France: information mentioned in a manuscript. To a questionnaire dating probably from 1907, quoted in the Notre Dame de France archives. 52
88. Article signed A. Lacordaire, published in La Semaine Catholique de Lyon [The Catholic Week of Lyons], June 1868.
89. Since 1954 the church, situated in rue de Conservatoire in the 9th district, has been re-baptised St. Eugene and St. Cecilia, patron of musicians, so as to recall the proximity of the Music Conservatory in Paris.
90. An article in the The Architect and Building News, 13 February 1942 p. 132 and 138 mentions three rose windows, one over the main altar, and one over each of the side altars.
91. Extract from an article dated 11th June 1868 in an English newspaper (title not found).
92. Quoted in the booklet Notre Dame de France, 1965, p.12.
93. Aristide Cavaillé-Coll (1811-1899).
94. This is a two-manual organ with twenty-four sets.
95. John Henry Newman (1801-1890).
96. Henry Manning (1808-1892).
97. Eugène Viollet-le-Duc (1814-1879).
98. Such as Sunday Vespers, retreats, liturgical vestments…
99. 70 young girls were enrolled.
100. The small Panorama behind the Rotonde, facing Ryder's Court, near Leicester Court, has disappeared.
101. Opened in 1861 on Regent Street by Dr. Vintras and the perfumer Rimmel.
102. In 18 Lisle Street, a rented building, then in No 34-35, a building acquired by the Marist Fathers.
103. 200 m from there. The hospital would work at this address until 1965. A French convalescent home was built in Brighton in 1895 for patients leaving hospital and for the elderly.
104. Or freehold. The date for the expiry of the lease was 1890.
105. 1865-1874 and 1876-1881. Father Faure had been recalled to Paris by the Marists in 1874, replaced in the interval. He returned to Paris in 1881 where he died seven years later.
106. It covered the church, the girls' school, 5 Leicester Place and two nearby houses, No.'s 4 and 6 Leicester Place.
107. The Superiors of Notre Dame de France from the foundation are listed at the end of the book.

108. Father Jean Thomas (1883-1915) superior from 1883 to 1888 and from 1892 to 1898, see the booklet Notre Dame de France 1965, p.39.
109. A. Poncet s.m. Booklet Notre Dame de France, 1965, p.17.
110. Extract from an article in The Daily Graphic, 3rd July 1894. A no less grandiose ceremony will take place in Notre Dame de France after the death of President Félix Faure in 1899.
111. Father Jean-Baptiste Gay (1861-1940) Superior from 1903 to 1911 and from 1921 to 1927. See booklet: Notre Dame de France, 1965 p. 39.
112. A. Poncet s.m. Booklet Notre Dame de France in London, p.43.
113. Quoted in the booklet Notre Dame de France 1965 p. 17.
114. Law voted 9th December 1905 at the initiative of socialist republican Aristide Briand (1862-1932), member of the French parliament.
115. Paul Cambon (1843-1924), Ambassador in London from 1898 to 1920.
116. Francois Batisse. Notes on the L'église catholique française de Londres [French Catholic Church in London], London 1973.
117. Signed on 8th April 1904, the Entente Cordiale is a series of bilateral agreements intended to put an end to the colonial rivalries of the two countries. It is the basis for the Triple Alliance with Russia, supposed to control diplomatically the rise to power of Germany.
118. Father Maxime Robin (1861-1945) Superior from 1911 to 1921 see booklet: Notre Dame de France, 1965 p. 40.
119. Demand did not cease and it was necessary to move again: from 1930 the Lycée would occupy the actual site of today.
120. Other French established themselves before them, the Huguenots in the 17th century, then the Royalists in the 18th century.
121. Girls' school: 124 students, boys' school: 120 students, crèche: 108 children.
122. After a first summer camp in 1907, Baden Powell created the Scout movement, but it was only on 25th July 1920 that the Fédération Nationale Catholique des Scouts de France [National Catholic Federation of Scouts of France] was born officially.
123. Father Laurent (1876-1948).
124. Eric Simon, Londres au fil de la France libre [London following Free France], Keswick editions, 2013 p.11.
125. Paul Morand, head of the economic mission, joins the government of Vichy and André Maurois leaves for USA.
126. Memoirs of Suzanne Boissieux, quoted by Eric Simon, 2013, p.102.
127. During this period London was bombed 71 times by the Luftwaffe 57 nights in a row.
128. Eric Simon, 2013, p.5 and p.6.
129. In fact at 20.45.
130. The exact source was not found. Quoted in the Booklet Notre Dame de France 1965, p.19 and 20.
131. Diary of Father Laurent.
132. Words of Colonel Rémy quoted by Colonel Passy in the article: L'épopée d'agents secrets qui n'avaient que leur courage [The epic of the secret agents who had only their courage], June 1960, publication not found.
133. Diary of Father Laurent
134. Notes of Father Paul Ginisty at the Society of Mary in Paris around 1946, Provincial Archives Paris Doc 451127.
135. Notes of the Rector Laurent at the Society of Mary in Paris around 1942, Provincial Archives Paris Doc 420824. 53

136. In fact only the girls' school is open.
137. Notes of the Rector Laurent at the Society of Mary in Paris around 1942, Provincial Archives Paris Doc 420324.
138. Maurice Schumann (1911-1998).
139. Words of Colonel Rémy reported by Colonel Passy in an article « L'épopée d'agents secrets qui n'avaient que leur courage » [The epic of secret agents who had only their courage] June 1960, unidentified publication.
140. Sculptor Henri Valette (1891-1962).
141. Contract for shipping of goods.
142. Bishop Myers, auxiliary bishop of Westminster.
143. Fr. Francois Laurent, Rector of Notre Dame de France from 1933- 1947.
144. Words of Colonel Rémy reported by Colonel Passy in an article « L'épopée d'agents secrets qui n'avaient que leur courage » [The epic of secret agents who had only their courage] June 1960.
145. In the first church, the statue measuring 2.10 m, was above the main altar.
146. Notes of Father Paul Ginisty at the Society of Mary in Paris around 1946, Provincial Archives Paris Doc 451127.
147. Fr. Guy Vernert, sermon in memory of Fr. Gerard Noblet, Notre Dame de France, 11 May 2012.
148. See booklet Notre Dame de France 1965, p.20.
149. Notes of Yves Le Creurer given by him to the archives of Notre Dame de France 1999.
150. Anthony Eden (1897-1977).
151. Ambassador of France from 1944 to 1955.
152. Father Francisque Deguerry (1883-1953) parish priest of Notre Dame de France from 1948 to 1953, former missionary in Tonga.
153. René Varin (1896-1976).
154. From the cabinet of Corfiato architects, Steward Lloyd Thomson and Partners.
155. Jean-Charles Moreaux (1889-1956).
156. Cardinal Feltin.
157. Cardinal Griffin.
158. An unsigned article cut out of an unidentified daily newspaper, October 1955.
159. Quoted in the booklet Notre Dame de France 1965, p.30.
160. Cardinal Griffin.
161. Father Couturier (1897-1954), Dominican, was Director of the review L'Art Sacré [Sacred Art] from 1935 to 1954.
162. Matisse for the Chapel in Vance, Cocteau for the chapels in Villefranche- sur-Mer and Notre Dame de France in London, the two greatest names of the French avant-garde: Braque, Chagall, Leger, Lurcat, Matisse, Rouault and others for the church in Plateau d'Assy in Haute Savoie, Le Corbusier for the chapel in Ronchamp in Haute-Saône.
163. A canvas plaque sewn on the back of the tapestry has this inscription: "Notre Dame de France H. 5.3m L .4.5m, cartoon of Dom Robert de Chaunac, edited by Tabard Brothers and Sisters, Aubusson.
164. Jean Lurcat (1892-1966) painter and tapestry cartoonist who contributed to the renewal of the art of tapestry from 1930 onwards.
165. Excerpt from a text of Dom Robert « Composition d'un carton de tapisserie » [Composition of a tapestry cartoon] in a catalogue of his exposition in the Galerie La Demeure, Paris, 1974.
166. Because of successive cleanings and the discolouration of the blue pigment by the light, the bottom of the tapestry today is a clear brown colour.

167. Georges Saupique (1899-1961).
168. Mandorle comes from the Latin mandorla: almond.
169. One of the Virgin "prototypes" found especially in the Eastern Church.
170. Emile Stoll (1908-1961).
171. His name has not been found.
172. Boris Anrep (1883-1969).
173. Excerpt from an article by Boris Anrep in Echo of Notre Dame de France, June/July 1955.
174. For Mary.
175. Later the tabernacle will be moved to the baptismal font, on the side opposite the chapel painted by Cocteau in 1956.
176. Stolen in 1986, never recovered.
177. Thanks to René Varin, Jean Cocteau (1889-1963) had been awarded Doctor Honoris Causa at the Oxford University in 1956.
178. Allusion to the wave of renewal touching Sacred Art after the Second World War.
179. Quotes from a speech given by René Varin the 25th March 1965, on the occasion of the centenary of Notre Dame de France. 54
180. The "us" refers to the Marist Fathers of Notre Dame de France at that time: Fathers Jacquemin, Rector, Bovar, Reyter and Le Creurer.
181. Father Yves Le Creurer's notes sent to the archivist in Notre Dame de France in 1999.
182. Father Yves Le Creurer's notes, see previous notes.
183. Oedipus Rex: opera-oratorio composed in 1927 by Igor Stravinsky on a French booklet of Jean Cocteau.
184. Excerpt of a letter from Father Jacquemin, Rector of Notre Dame de France to the Marist Provincial in Paris, London 18th May 1959.
185. One of the statues to be seen in the church Notre Dame de France.
186. Jean Cocteau's letter to Father Yves Le Creurer, November 1959.
187. The vase is garnished with white lilies – symbols of purity – and red carnations, symbols of commitment and conjugal fidelity.
188. Quoted in the notes of Father Le Creurer given in 1999 to the archivist in Notre Dame De France.
189. Cocteau was associated with the Ordre de la Rose-Croix Catholique et Esthétique du Temple et du Graal [Order of the Catholic and Aesthetic Rose Cross of the Temple and the Grail]. This artistic movement of right-wing Catholicism, had broken away from the Kabbalistic Rose Cross.
190. One sometimes associates the falcon with the victory of light over darkness.
191. The fish is a symbol of Christ.
192. Report of G. and L. Scoupe, a single document, unidentified publication, 1955.
193. The rector is Fr. Deguerry. Quoted in the booklet Notre Dame de France, London, 1965, p.27.
194. Henri de Lubac (1896-1991).
195. Maurice Zundel (1897-1975).
196. Jean Daniélou, (1905-1974).
197. Jacques de Bollardière (1907-1986).
198. Charles Péguy Centre, 114-116 Curtain Road, London EC2A 3AH.
199. Created in France in 1941 by Marie Louise Monet (1902-1988) sister of John, founder of the Europe, the ACI regrouped teams of lay people linked with priests for apostolic purposes. Its mission was to evangelise people with independent backgrounds: to evangelise similar people by similar people, by calling them to re-read their lives in the light of the

NOTES

200. Father Henri Caffarel (1903-1996) on the spirituality of Christian marriage.
201. In 1951.
202. St Vincent de Paul Conference. Founded in 1833 in Paris by Frédéric Ozanam from Lyon (1813-1853) for the purpose of helping those most in need.
203. Document addressed by Notre Dame de France to the Consulate General in London, March 1960.
204. The Welcoming Committee and the Coordination for the Integration of the Mauritians (CACIM).
205. Present in Notre Dame de France from 1962-1966.
206. Personal notes of Jean Murat, London, September 2014.
207. John Heenan (1905-1975) Archbishop of Westminster from 1963 until his death.
208. Personal notes of Jean Murat, London, September 2014.
209. Present in Notre Dame de France from 1966 to 1987, Father Francois Groetz replaced Father Raabe in 1966.
210. Andre Huguet s.m. in 'Service National et Cooperation', not dated, around 1962-65.
211. René Varin had recommended the architect and then the artists who decorated the church rebuilt after the war. The former Cultural Advisor to the embassy became the Inspector General of State Education.
212. By the organist Nicole Pillet.
213. Bishop John Heenan.
214. (1884-1973) Bishop of Lille and President of the Cardinals and Bishops of France.
215. Bishop Igino Cardinale.
216. In 1968.
217. Notably Pastor Dubois from the Protestant parish in Soho, the Catholic Ukrainian bishop, an Anglican Benedictine bishop and a Pastor of the Swiss church.
218. Quoted by Jean Bourdarias: The visit of the Archbishop of Paris to England, article in the Figaro, 21st February 1970.
219. Personal notes of Colette Moran, London, September 2014.
220. In December 1965.
221. Personal notes of Father Gerard Noblet 2008.
222. Personal notes of Father Gerard Noblet 2008.
223. Michel Rigal.
224. Personal notes of Father Gerard Noblet 2008.
225. Situated at Queen's Gate, beside the Lycée, it offers the use of a guest house and meeting rooms to every unit of the movement from any country.
226. Father Wernert arrived in Notre Dame de France in 1979 and worked for two years with Frs Gerard Noblet and Joel Bozon before becoming Rector from 1981 to 1986.
227. Sermon of Father Guy Wernert in the remembrance Mass for Father Noblet, Notre Dame de France, 11 May 2012.
228. A level is a class, which changes every year.
229. 59 Brook Green, London W6 7BE in the West of the city. The JP school is subsidised at present.
230. Situated in Shaftsbury Avenue.
231. In 1966.
232. In 1967 the British Minister for Health bought back the building renamed Shaftsbury Hospital. While the medical services were associated with the hospitals of St. Peter, St. Paul and St. Philip, the Shaftsbury Hospital would be absorbed in 1992 in what would be known as the Middlesex Hospital.

233. Fleet Street where a good number of journalists are based was not far away.
234. The DGAFE is part of the Department of the Universal Mission of the Conference of the Bishops of France. Its work is to support and appoint pastors for all the Catholic, French Chaplaincies in the world.
235. Father Jovenez had just finished. He did not shed his pastoral mandate in the French parish in Vienna (Austria).
236. Yolande Cantu died of illness in 1998.
237. Conversation of the author with Maria Refig, London, 5th October 2014.
238. The Ambassador at the time is Luc de La Barre de Nanteuil, serving from 1986 to 1990.
239. Jacques Coupet received "Maxima cum laude" for his thesis which today is recognised as a work of reference.
240. He did not live in the presbytery and sometime got a replacement for the Sunday Mass.
241. In 2015 Maria Refig is still very active in the chaplaincy.
242. Situated north-east of the church, with a separate entrance in 34 Lisle Street.
243. The electric circuit of the console was replaced and the division system of the pedalboard was improved upon. Six stops were added derived from existing pipes.
244. Led by Father Paul Walsh and Pastor Stéphane Desmarais in 2015.
245. Christ Church, Victoria Road, London W8 5RQ.
246. A Marist of great spirituality.
247. In Norfolk.
248. Sister Helena, Sister Carmel, Sister Marie-Paule and Sister Catherine.
249. From December to March.
250. Night Shelter for the homeless, organised by the Churches Together in Westminster.
251. Succeeding Father Walsh during the Summer 1999, the directress is French but not a parishioner of Notre Dame de France. The third directress came from the Protestant church in Soho.
252. The text of the Trust was officially modified in 2005.
253. International Centre of Exchange.
254. First Marist martyr in Oceania in 1841.
255. St. Patrick's – Soho Square, Corpus Christi – Covent Garden, Our Lady of the Assumption and St. Gregory – Warwick Street and Notre Dame de France.
256. Cardinal Vincent Nichols.
257. The Jeweller's Shop in 2011.
258. Kolbe's Gift in 2013.
259. With Saltmine Theatre.
260. Burkina Faso, Cameroon, Canada, Democratic Republic of Congo, France, Ivory Coast, Madagascar, Mali, Mauritius, Senegal, Switzerland and Togo. The flags were put there in 2012 at the time of the London Olympic Games.

The Rectors of Notre Dame de France since the foundation

Charles Faure s.m.	1865 – 1874 and 1876 – 1881
Jean-Louis Rocher s.m.	1874 – 1875
Jean Leterrier s.m.	1875 – 1876
Jean-Baptiste Petitalot s.m.	1881 – 1884
Jean Thomas s.m.	1883 – 1888 and 1892 – 1898
Augustin Aubry s.m.	1888 – 1889
Louis de Mijolla s.m.	1889 – 1892
Edmond Charrier s.m.	1899 – 1903
Jean-Baptiste Gay s.m.	1903 – 1911 and 1921 – 1927
Maxime Robin s.m.	1911 – 1921
Louis Perrot s.m.	1927 – 1933
François Laurent s.m.	1933 – 1947
Adolphe Rabel s.m.	1947 – 1948
Francisque Deguerry s.m.	1948 – 1953
Paul Jacquemin s.m.	1953 – 1962
André Huguet s.m.	1962 – 1968
Gérard Noblet s.m.	1968 – 1981
Guy Wernert s.m.	1981 – 1987
Raymond Jovenez	1987 – 1989 Diocesan priest of Paris
Jacques Coupet o.p.	1989 – 1992
Clive Birch s.m.	1992 – 1996
John Collier s.m.	1996 – 1999
Bernard Boisseau s.m.	1999 – 2002
Martin McAnaney s.m.	2002 – 2004
Joaquín Fernández s.m.	2004 – 2008
Paul Walsh s.m.	2008 – 2015
Pascal Boidin s.m.	2015 –

Bibliography

Chassaigne, Philippe, Histoire de l'Angleterre des origines à nos jours, collection Champs Histoire, Flammarion, Paris 2008

Cordier, Daniel, Alias Caracalla, collection Folio, Gallimard, Paris 2009

Étèvenaux, Jean, Français et Britanniques, collection L'àpart de l'esprit, Fabrica Libri, Turquant 2010

Janvrin, Isabelle et Catherine Rawlinson, Les Français à Londres de Guillaume Le Conquérant à Charles de Gaulle, Bibliomane, Paris 2013

Jaulmes, Yves, The French Protestant Church and the Huguenots, Église Protestante Française de Londres, 1993

Murdoch, Tessa, The Quiet Conquest, The Huguenots 1685-1985, exhibition catalogue, Museum of London, London 15 May – 31 October 1985

Paxman, Jeremy, The English, Penguin, London 1999

Pepys, Samuel, Journal 1660-1669, Collection Le Temps retrouvé, Mercure de France, Paris 2007

Pevsner, Nikolaus, The Buildings of England: London Vol. 6 Westminster, Yale University Press 2003

Reclus, Élisée, Guide du voyageur à Londres et aux environs, Guides Joanne, Hachette, Paris 1860, e-book

Rémy, Colonel (alias Renault Gilbert), Mémoires d'un agent secret de la France libre, tome 1 éditions de Crémille, Genève 1990. Tome 3, France Empire, Paris 1998

Simon, Éric, Londres au fil de la France libre, Keswick, London 2013

Soyez, Jean-Marc, Quand les Anglais vendangeaient l'Aquitaine, Fayard, Paris 1978

Tombs, Robert and Isabelle, That Sweet Enemy, Pimlico, London 2007

BULLETINS, PERIODICALS AND JOURNALS

Aprile, Sylvie, Translations politiques et culturelles : les proscrits français et l'Angleterre, in revue Genèse No 38, March 2000

Bulletin de la Colonie française à Londres (Bulletin of the French colony in London)

ECPDA (Établissement de communication et de production audiovisuelle pour la Défense) archives, Naissance de la France libre 18 juin 1940

Hamonet, Alfred, Annuaire commercial et industriel des français en Angleterre, W. Jeffs, London 1862

Lefebvre, Michel, 1940 La débâcle et l'espoir, Le Monde, Special issue, May – June 2010

PARISH ARCHIVES OF NOTRE DAME DE FRANCE

Batisse, François, Notes de conférences sur l'histoire de Notre Dame de France, Londres 1973

Copies of letters addressed to civil and religious authorities (Society of Mary and others)

CORRESPONDENCE

Estimates and miscellaneous documents referring to the building and rebuilding of the church

Files on parish activities and the works of art located in the church

Inventories and lists

Parish registers

Personal diaries

Press articles (general and religious, in French and English)

Title deeds

Two booklets on the history of Notre Dame de France, London 1923, 1965